Sky Falling
How to Overcome a Rogue Day

Paul Roland

authorHOUSE®

AuthorHouse™
1663 Liberty Drive, Suite 200
Bloomington, IN 47403
www.authorhouse.com
Phone: 1-800-839-8640

© 2008 Paul Roland. All rights reserved.

No part of this book may be reproduced, stored in a retrieval system, or transmitted by any means without the written permission of the author.

First published by AuthorHouse 11/17/2008

ISBN: 978-1-4389-3474-7 (sc)

Printed in the United States of America
Bloomington, Indiana

This book is printed on acid-free paper.

"These things have I spoken unto you, that in me ye might have peace. In the world ye shall have trials and tribulations: but be of good cheer; I have overcome the world."

JESUS CHRIST
John 16:33

I would like to dedicate this book to my dear mother, Peggy Montalvo, who confronted her own rogue day with courage and faith in Jesus Christ. Mom, I miss you still.

Contents

Introduction: Sky Falling ix

1. Unlock a Joyful Attitude 1
2. Unlock an Understanding Mind 21
3. Unlock a Surrendered Will.. 39
4. Unlock a Heart That Wants to Believe 49
5. The Rogue Day Called Death 59
6. What Is Death Like? 77
7. Heaven: The Journey Home.. 81

Conclusion.. 129
End Notes... 131

INTRODUCTION

Sky Falling

How to Overcome a Rogue Day

"Ouch, my head hurts!"

In the original "1943" story *Chicken Little*, Chicken Little was hit on the head by an acorn. Thereafter, he came to the conclusion that the sky was falling. So, what did he do? Chicken Little gathered his friends (Turkey Lurky, Loosey Goosey, Flemming Lemming) and he led them through the community heralding the warning, "The sky is falling. The sky is falling." In the end, a sly and sympathetic Foxey Loxley enticed them into a cave. There they met a carnivorous end.

The sudden and unexpected thud of the acorn on a cranium pavement did not mean the sky was falling; it only set-off emotional reactions that made it seem the sky was falling. That is exactly the way it appears when the trials of life unexpectedly rise up to threaten our fragile existence.

We are predisposed to run in circles, much like a chicken with his head chopped-off, looking for a place to hide. Emotionally we have convinced ourselves the sky is falling and life is over.

The more important lesson is realized in Foxey Loxley, a symbol for evil. Such as it is, we live in a dangerous, evil, world-environment where a stealth-like evil ever stalks its prey.[1] Your life can be challenged, controlled, contorted, and victimized. The question of fairness should not enter the equation of mastering evil, though people readily invoke "the-God-is-not-fair" hypothesis when the misfortunes of life come knocking. Misfortune, a sky falling, a rogue day, call it what you will. But life is what it is: Imperfect and blighted with a rabid evil. And every human being is susceptible to this universal harbinger. No one is immune.

Evil can consume us just like a Foxey Loxley. But unlike Chicken Little, wisdom from God's Word can equip us mentally, emotionally, and spiritually to be prepared. Our faith in Jesus Christ is paramount. Do remember, please, that The Son of God allowed himself to be bruised by evil.[2] But on the third day when the God-man rose from the dead—evil, wide-eyed and bewildered, slithered away crushed to its very core.[3] No small wonder Jesus could say, "...but be of good cheer; *I have overcome the world*."[4] Faith in Christ by His finished work on the cross is our victory over the "Foxey Loxley" who presently wields dominion over this world.

Rogue Day Events

Now, let us put another spin on these "sky-falling" events

Of life, or what we will call "rogue days." Rogue days are adverse episodes in life that make you feel like the sky is falling. It is some life-trial that you believe is inescapable and destructive. And it very well could be destructive. But many times life-trials are meant to act as an alarm, a warning, that the world is indeed a dangerous place to walk alone. . . without God.[5]

Have you ever heard of a *rogue wave?*

Mariners call these nonnegotiable waves "rogue waves," or "freak seas."[6] In Sebastian Junger's book, "The Perfect Storm," he characterized them as "Typically very steep and having an equally steep trough in front of them——a 'hole in the ocean' as some witnesses have described them."[7] These are monster waves that come out of no where and have the power to destroy a ship and its crew, which as the author said happened to the ill-fated *Andrea Gail*.

When a ship encounters a rogue wave that exceeds its stress rating the results can be disastrous. Ships encountering this danger find that they cannot get their bows up fast enough and the monster wave breaks their back. Blue water floods the hull. The boat and crew suffer the fate of a watery grave at the bottom of the ocean floor. Junger says:

> *"Maritime history is full of encounters with such waves. When Sir Ernest Shackleton was forced to cross the south-polar Sea in a twenty-two-foot open life boat, he saw a wave so big that he mistook its foaming crest for a moonlit cloud. He had only time to yell, "Hang on, boys, it's got us!" before the wave broke over his boat."*[8]

He continues to tell us:

> "The biggest rogue on record was during a Pacific gale in 1933, when the 478-foot Navy tanker Rampo was on her way from Manila to San Diego. She encountered a massive low-pressure system that blew up to sixty-eight knots for a week straight and resulted in a fully developed sea that the Rampo had no choice but to take on her stern. (Unlike today's tankers, the Rampo's wheelhouse was slightly forward of amidships.) Early on the morning of February seventh, the watch officer glanced to stern and saw a freak wave rising up behind him that lined up perfectly with a crow's nest above and behind the bridge. Simple geometry later showed the wave to be 112 feet high."[9]

Sometimes these Frankenstein freaks of nature come in a trilogy called "the three sisters." These are multiple waves that somehow happen to get "in step" forming highly unstable piles of water.[10]

Can you imagine being in a boat on a calm sea? You are enjoying the "perfect" day. There is the gentle lapping of water against the hull. There are pelicans, as if sketched by an unseen hand, gliding across the azure horizon. A gentle wind moves your craft from stern to bow, just enough to generate a tranquility that makes the eyes heavy. Then it happens. A 90-degree wall of water rising 112 feet high from the sea with blind vengeance. There is no time to run and hide, even if you could. At 80 miles an hour, the rogue wave, like a fast elevator, lifts your boat to the crest and in its grip of destruction you only have time to taste the salt spray and scream.

What Is a Rogue Day?

Rogue waves are serious business, but so are *rogue days*. "Rogue days," you say. "What is a rogue day?" A rogue day translates into the unexpected trials of life that brings disaster and chaos into our fragile lives. And rogue days can travel in "threes."

It was September 26, 2006, when the phone rang shortly after lunch. On the other end was Charles Henderson. "Did you hear?" he asked.

"Hear what?" I replied.

"Chad Harris was killed at work this morning. He fell three stories while fitting a window with a glass pane."

"How did you hear?" I said.

"It happened this morning. It's been on the news most of the day," Charles said.

"I can't believe it. I just can't believe it."

There was a lull in the conversation and then Charles said: "You know what they say? It always comes in *threes*."

Earlier in the year, Chad's wife had lost her brother to cancer and now Chad. Their lives had become a house of sorrows for the foreseeable future. The white backwash of a rogue day always leaves in its wake hopeless despair.

We have all had difficult days that were a physical/spiritual challenge. And when bad things happen, we can expect the physical and the spiritual dimensions of our nature to intersect and affect each other. Physical suffering will invite spiritual anguish, and vice-versa. Who of us has not groaned in the spirit when we were sick in the body, or emotionally wounded?

A few years ago, I suffered in the body with the flu for ten days. I ached with pain and fever. It afflicted every part of my body. If you don't think my spirit was in anguish, just ask the one who tried to take care of me, my wife. Sad to say, I did not suffer graciously in my spirit. Indeed, I was not good company. If you hurt in the body, the spirit also will suffer; if you suffer in the spirit, then the body can literally get sick. The body and the spirit/soul of man work closely with one another.[11]

We see this activity in the life of our Lord when he prayed in the Garden of Gethsemane that the cup of suffering be removed. And we are told: "...being in agony he prayed more earnestly: And his sweat was like great drops of blood falling down to the ground."[12] The spiritual oppression that our Lord experienced was manifested through a bodily response, the blood. In the scheme of God's design for man, you cannot have one without the other; that is, bodies without spirit/soul involvement and vice-versa. And so, we see here a connection between the essential dichotomies of man.

If we know this interconnection of body and spirit/soul, then we should also recognize how important it is to experience the joy of the Presence of the Lord.[13] The strength to overcome adversity is not in the body, although the body is fearfully and wondrously made.[14] The body indeed was designed with curative powers, or else one could never overcome sickness. And medication can help the healing process, or stabilize emotional trauma.[15] But Strength to overcome the adversity of a rogue event, whatever the trial, is best manifested as we focus on the joy of the Presence of the Lord. The results will be a spirit of joy which generates the Peace of God that no matter the trial, you are not alone. In your storm, there is one who walks on the tempest-tossed and is able to say to a rogue day, *Peace be still*.[16]

But in this life, rogue days appear to come out of a no where. They are so sudden, so fierce. Sometimes you think it can not happen to you. You think it will always happen to the other guy, the one with a nameless face. But no one is immune to the trials of life. And so we must learn that "God is no respecter of persons."[17] It is only by the grace of God if one suffers less, or more. And it is not "if" trials will come, but simply a matter of "when." Like a rogue wave, the trials of life will rise up and suddenly you find yourself in the path of an all consuming wall of despair and destruction.

Joy abandons you.

Hope drowns.

Defeat like an angry wave cresting, seeks your total devastation.

Life, such as it is, will be pitted with calamities; that is, we live in a world where at any given moment we may fall victim to ruin. We might well liken our journey along Pilgrim's Way as a highway littered with IED's(Internal Explosive Devices), the kind of bombs we hear terrorists like to use against our troops in Iraq; bombs you can not see till it is too late. These well-hidden explosives are just waiting to cripple or kill unsuspecting travelers.

On April 16, 2007, Cho Seung-Hui set out on his grim task of accomplishing the deadliest shooting in modern

U.S. history. Virginia Tech University in Blacksburg, Virginia would be his target. Sick with the poison of malice and madness, this crazed "would-be" murderer lay in his bed staring at the ceiling and staging the next day's frightful massacre. "I'll kill 'em...I'll kill 'em all," Cho snarled. His was a vile soul, vile as the poetry that dribbled outside his lunatic mind. "Tomorrow," he gloated with a fiendish groan, "I will write my poetry from the blood of every soul that crosses my path." Cho had crossed the line from whence there is no return. He was human in form only. His soul was thoroughly possessed. He had become raw evil and tomorrow anarchy would reign. There would be no warning. People would surely die. And people did die, thirty-two students who could never have imagined how the last day of their lives would be played-out.

We do not know what lies ahead of us from one day to the next. The believer must be prepared at all times for the heart-wrenching events of life. It is not only the approach, but also the aftermath of a rogue day. And if a certain rogue event means our demise, then another preparation is in order: We must be prepared to meet the God with whom we have to do. It was Amos the Prophet who warned Israel: "...prepare to meet thy God, O Israel."[18]

On any given day that we rise to greet the sun, it could be our last day on earth. We live in just this kind of chaotic world where anything can happen. How many times do we read of a young life lost in an automobile accident? It is so tragic, so sad. Or, freak accidents that take a life? Just today, in the Mobile Register, two brother-n-laws in their early twenties were killed when their truck ran off the road and hit a tree. One of them had only been married for six weeks. No one sets out into the day thinking they are going to die, but it happens. Who can know the challenges of one day in a life? Jesus said in Matthew 6:34: "...sufficient unto the day is the evil thereof."

December 11, 2006, I prayed with a fearful mother over the phone, her thirty-nine year old baby girl just suffered a heart-attack. Teresa couldn't breathe; her left arm was aching as she rose from her sleep. Soon she was on her way to the emergency room of the Providence Hospital. How could this happen to such a young person? Teresa was too young to die. Her whole life was before her. What about her children? Or, her husband? This couldn't be happening, not to this dear mother with so many years ahead. This rogue experience came out of nowhere. In the backwash of this event was fear and spiritual turmoil, but prayers were answered and Teresa was delivered.

Rogue days are real and call for a plan of action. And the question that begs an answer is: Are you spiritually prepared to experience a rogue day? Most are not.

Two Kinds of Rogue Days

Jesus warned that we should be proactive to our own spiritual preparation against a rogue day. He cited two rogue events and the necessity of soul preparation:

"There were present at that season some that told Him of the Galileans, whose blood Pilate had mingled with their sacrifices. And Jesus answering said unto them,

> *Suppose ye that these Galileans were sinners above all the Galileans, because they suffered such things? I tell you, nay: but, except you repent, ye shall all likewise perish. Or those*

> eighteen, upon whom the tower in Siloam fell, and slew them, think ye that they were sinners above all men that dwell in Jerusalem? I tell you, Nay: but, except ye repent, ye shall all likewise perish."[19]

The background to these passages concerned two rogue events: Pilate had the Galileans, who represent *moral suffering*, murdered while they sacrificed animals for worship. And then there was the tower that collapsed and killed eighteen construction workers which represent *natural suffering*. Herein are the two types of suffering we can expect as creatures who live in a rogue environment. Either you suffer an immoral act forced by another, or simply find yourself in the wrong place, at the wrong time, which brings natural suffering.

Since Cain murdered Abel millions have been killed at the hand of their brother or sister. It may have been in a time of war or some murderous act. But the killing of a human unleashes moral suffering upon the innocent. And as for natural suffering, had you chanced to be in New Orleans, Louisiana, on August 29, 2005, doubtless you would have suffered simply because you happened to be in the city when Hurricane Katrina ravaged the area. We need to prepare ourselves for the inherent suffering that an imperfect world can bring, a world plagued by rogue days. And above all, never blame God for a world we chose for ourselves, a world blemished with both moral and natural rogue events.

As Jews believed that suffering was connected with sin, they wanted to know what thought Jesus had on the two tragedies. Our Lord cut across the current belief of the day and confronted the truth that calamity is no respecter of persons. "No," Jesus said, "but, except you repent, you shall all likewise perish."

In this perilous life, where anything that can happen will happen, we need to be prepared to meet our Maker; that is, to be sure that we have peace with God through the blood of the cross of Jesus Christ.[20] Soul-preparation against the aftermath of any rogue day is to "repent and believe the Gospel."[21] Ours is a haphazard life. Simply being in the wrong place at the wrong time invites destruction. Or, perhaps God allows evil to mark one for a rogue day. Job was divinely given a rogue day and allowed to suffer.[22] We must be prepared to meet a rogue day. And to meet God, if need be.

Life Is Not Fair

You say, "Well, that doesn't seem fair."

You are right. It is not fair. But then whoever said that life was going to be fair? It certainly was not God. God warned the first couple about going in a direction that was contrary to his will. We are told:

> *"And the Lord God commanded the man, saying, of every tree of the garden thou mayest freely eat. But the tree of the knowledge of good and evil, thou shalt not eat of it: for in the day that thou eatest thereof thou shalt surely die."*[23]

God said, "...thou shalt surely die." And, of course, the Bible tells us: "For since by man came death...For as in Adam all die...."[24]

God warned Adam and Eve that everything would change for the worst if they did not heed His warning. And as we know too well, death continues to advance and conquer physical life. No one is exempt from the penalty of our parent's first wrong choice. That infamous day the human race died physically and spiritually. It is only the grace of God that allows for our temporary existence, a short time for soul-preparation to get things right with God through the blood of the cross of the Lord Jesus. It is the blood that washes away our sins and brings reconciliation between God and Man.

But this death also suggests something else; it means that our environment has changed from one of divine security to the insecurity of living in a world where we are susceptible to rogue day events. In the garden paradise that God made for the first man and woman, they were secure in all things and enjoyed perfect bliss. There was divine fellowship, provision, and God's protection. Paradise was squandered when Adam chose to ignore the warning of God. To this very day, man still longs for paradise, a place of peace, security, and tranquility. But alas, what once was is no more. The way to primordial bliss has been barred and a flaming sentry guards the entrance.[25]

Do you remember the dying thief beside the cross of the Lord Jesus? In his last hour of earthly life, he dreamed of paradise. And He, who knows the intent of every heart, bruised as he was, lifted his head off his swollen breast and inhaled sufficient breath to speak the words, "Today thou shall be with me in *paradise*."[26] In the atoning work of Christ at the cross, paradise is no longer barred. No longer is paradise a wishful thought, but a present reality to those who call on his name for salvation. Our eternal security has been restored, but only through the blood of the silent sufferer.

Now, at the risk of sounding simplistic and crude—— *stuff just happens*. And it is a moral expediency that we are prepared at all times to meet God.

Point in Case: He lived in Nickel Mines, Pennsylvania. His name was Charles Carl Martin, a thirty year old milkman who had just finished his morning route at four o'clock. Later he took his children to the bus stop, he wanted to make sure they were safe and on their way to school. Then he turned his attention to the one-room, Amish schoolhouse where shortly he would molest and kill five young girls, none over the age of thirteen. In less than an hour, he too, would be standing before His Maker.

Were these girls suffering for some terrible sin that they should be murdered by a crazed killer? No, a thousand times we say no. These precious little girls were tragic victims of living in an immoral and insecure world where evil at any given moment may raise its hoary head. That's why Jesus said: "I Tell you, no: But, except ye repent, ye shall all likewise perish."[27] In an insecure world, we must be prepared to stand in the presence of God; we never know when our last day will arrive, or how it will come.

I was just a little boy running across the street in Kingsville, Texas, when I was hit by a car. In those days a car was a car. No plastic, it was all steel, and had goliath-sized tires. The impact knocked me out cold as a block of ice. Dad pulled my head from under the huge chrome bumper. Just inches closer and my little head would have been . . . well, let us just say, flat as a fetter. The Lord, of course saved me. He interceded. Why? He had plans for my life. God, one day up the road, was to call me to preach the Gospel of Jesus Christ. Had things turned out differently, this could have been my last day on earth. That accident could have been my rogue day. Apparently, accomplishing God's purpose for our lives has a lot to do with divine intervention. There can be divine deliverance when one is at the mercy of a rogue event. Divine purposes cannot be aborted by evil. Nevertheless, we need to be ready. Jesus said "repent." This is the kind of world in which we live: A world and life we chose, so long ago, when we said *no* to God.

In his book "Riding With the Blue Moth," Bill Hancock, an administrator NCAA men's basketball tournament announcer and director of the NCAA Final Four Basketball tournament, knows the misery and anguish of the rogue day. His much beloved 31-year-old son, Will, who also worked in sport's journalism, was killed in a plane crash on January 27, 2001. Bill's rogue day went down like this:

> *At 10:00 p.m., we were startled awake by the ringing telephone. In the darkness, we could not find the receiver. The answering machine switched on and we heard Nellie Perry, Nicki's mother, speaking. Nellie's voice had been weakened by Parkinson's disease, but on this night it was particularly strong and hysterical.*

"Will was on the plane," Nellie cried. "Will's plane has crashed in Colorado."

As I fumbled to find the light switch, Nicki collapsed onto the floor shrieking, "Not Will. Not Will. Oh, please God, not Will."

She tucked her body into a fetal position, as if to protect her heart, then reached out and pounded her fist on the carpet. [28]

The colossal impact of this rogue event nearly destroyed Bill Hancock. He said:

"I tried to go for a run but halted on a country road, in tears. Running was too familiar, too hopeful, too ordinary. Simple habits, long-ingrained, became puzzles. I forgot the steps in brushing my teeth. Phone numbers and the names of acquaintances eluded me. Life's customs from music to work to attending church became draining emotional distractions. The great hymns made me weep. So Nicki and I moved from our customary spot in the third row to the back of the Ashbury Methodist sanctuary. There we had privacy and a quick escape route when the tears came, as they did every Sunday."[29]

Things did not get better:

> "I was spiraling out of control, feeling claustrophobic in a lonely room without doors or windows. There was no hope for the future, no reason to live, nowhere to go. My worst moments occurred when I considered how the lives of Nicki, Karen, and Nate had been wrecked; none of them deserved such pain: 'Put one foot in front of the other. Heaven is real. Will is there.' I'm not sure that I really believed any of it, but I chanted hard, pounding the hope into my head like a blacksmith wielding a hammer."[30]

How did Bill Hancock overcome his rogue day? For starters, he decided to ride his bike across the under belly of the southern regions of the United States. His journey began in Huntington Beach, California, and ended in Tybee Island, Georgia, a distance of 2,746 miles. Along the way, Bill soon came to realize that "God had sent a series of angels," in the form of special people to help him learn something about himself, and about life from his journey. He said:

> "I continued to find new meaning in the bike ride. For years, my prayer each evening had been 'Lord, make me an instrument of your peace.' But I didn't know how to be one. Then I realized that others are similarly untrained and naive but serve as agents of peace anyway. For example, Steve, in McRae, Georgia, didn't know he was my Peach Angel. He was just a regular guy doing his job, an unintentional angel."[31]

Somewhere along Bill's journey, he discovered the joy of the Presence of the Lord. And *He* was enough.

We have all had some really bad days that were difficult; we might call them hard-to-bare days; the kind of days that made you feel hopeless, defeated, and utterly miserable.

Perhaps you have heard of the poor man who was injured at work. When the insurance company sent a letter and asked him to clarify a few points, he responded:

> *"Dear Sir: I am writing in response to your request for additional information. In block 3, of the accident report form, I put poor planning as the cause of my accident. You said in your letter that I should explain more fully and so I trust that the following details will be sufficient.*
>
> *I am a bricklayer by trade. On the day of the accident I was working alone on the roof of a 6-story building. When I completed my work, I discovered that I had about 500 lbs. of bricks left over. Rather than carry the bricks down by hand, I decided to lower them in a barrel by using a pulley which, fortunately, was attached to the side of the building at the 6th floor. Securing the rope at ground level, I went up to the roof, swung the barrel, and loaded the bricks into it. Then I went back to the ground and untied the rope holding it tightly to ensure a slow descent of the 500 lbs. of bricks. You will notice in block 11, of the accident form, that I weigh 135 lbs.*

Now, due to my surprise at being jerked off the ground so suddenly, I lost my presence of mind and forgot to let go of the rope. Needless to say, I proceeded at a rapid rate up the side of the building. Somewhere in the vicinity of the 3-floor, I met the barrel coming down, This explains the fractured skull and collarbone. Slowing only slightly, I continued my rapid ascent, not stopping until the fingers of my right hand were deeply embedded in the pulley. Fortunately, by this time, I had received my presence of mind and was able to hold tightly to the rope in spite of my pain. At approximately the same time, however, the barrel of bricks hit the ground and the bottom fell out. Devoid of the weight of the bricks, the barrel now weighed approximately 50 lbs. I refer you again to my weigh in block 11. As you might imagine I began a rapid descent down the side of the building.

Now, somewhere in the vicinity of the 3-floor, I met the barrel coming up. This accounts for the 2 fractured ankles and the lacerations on my lower body and legs. The encounter with the barrel slowed me enough to lessen my injuries. Then I fell on the pile of bricks and fortunately, only 3 vertebrae were cracked.

I'm sorry to report, however, that as I lay there on the bricks, in pain, unable to stand, watching the empty barrel 6-stories above me,

> *I again lost my presence of mind. I let go of the rope."*

This is what we call a rogue day. It is a really bad day when Murphy's Law, "If anything can go wrong, it probably will," is working overtime. And it brings in its wake mental and spiritual anguish.

Have You Ever Had a Rogue Day?

Have you ever had a really bad day, a rogue day? Days that made you feel like God had taken a long vacation and Left you a message to "do the best you can?" We have all had times when things just didn't go right and it seemed the Lord left us all alone to manage the best we could. The Psalmist felt this way when he said: "Hide not Thy face far from me; put not thy servant away in anger; leave me not, neither forsake me, O God of my salvation."[32]

Take Paul the Apostle. There were plenty of days that were extremely lonely and difficult. One of the loneliest days of Paul's life was in a Roman prison awaiting his execution. He said: "For Demas hath forsaken me...only Luke is with me...Alexander the copper smith did me much evil...no man has stood with me...all men forsook me."[33]

This certainly was a rogue day for the dear apostle. Paul had been so faithful to his Lord, suffering all kinds of deprivations and heartaches for the cause of Christ. And look at him now: He was abandoned and forgotten. It was not fair. But wait! Hear what Paul said: "Notwithstanding the Lord stood with me and strengthened me..."[34] Paul, no doubt felt lonely as this rogue day of destruction drew near, but he definitely was not alone. His Master was in the prison cell ministering strength and peace to a chosen servant. Doubtless Paul was lonely, but he was definitely not alone.

God's people, no matter what circumstance of life, are never alone. The promise of His Presence is sufficient to bring comfort and courage to every bruised and broken heart.

Can you remember your last rogue day?

Maybe, your spouse of thirty years, without warning, asked you for a divorce. Or, a routine examination at the doctor's office revealed a dreaded cancer. Or, you were planning to retire from the company where you worked for 35-years, but there is a cutback and you're the first to go. Or, you get that call in the middle of the night that is every parent's dread; the voice on the other end of the line tells you that there has been an accident. Or, the bills have piled-up and you finally come to the stark realization that bankruptcy is the only way out.

We live in a world where rogue days happen to bad people, good people, and even God's people. And immunity from trials is not an option. Believers are not immune to rogue days. But the difference, in our time of troubles, is that we have the Presence of God to comfort us, prayer to empower us, and the Bible to instruct us how we can triumph over the rogue days that will surely come. For believers, reading the Bible, praying, and even suffering, is the way to develop intimacy with God. Suffering in the life of the believer has the unusual gravity of drawing us closer to the Lord. In John MacArthur's book, "The Power of Suffering," he wrote:

> *"In the context of suffering, therefore, we need to ask God for wisdom to help us persevere scripturally. We need His help to see sovereignty and providence working in our situation, to have a joyful attitude, and to respond submissively. This need for help dovetails marvelously with one of the overall purposes God has in allowing sufferings and trials: to make us more dependent on Him."*[35]

The peace of the Presence of God is what the believer seeks in the midst and aftermath of a rogue event.

How Can You Overcome a Rogue Day?

The key to overcoming those really difficult days is submission: Learn to *submit* yourself to the Lord and to the truth of scripture. The Bible says: "Submit yourself therefore to God. Resist the devil, and he will flee from you."[36]

Submission is the act of placing your trust in the authority of another. In context, we are speaking of "submissive faith." Submissive faith invites the miracle-working power of God into your life. Many people are content with a simple faith, a faith that harbors doubts concerning the reliability of God. But submissive faith is altogether different. No matter the crisis, God is able!

Luke, chapter 5, offers four examples of the effectiveness of submissive faith: First, Peter submitted to the authority of Christ's Word to "Launch out into the deep, and let down your nets for a draught." Peter caught so many fish it nearly swamped two boats. Next, a leper submitted to the authority of Christ's Word "Be thou clean," and he was healed. A man sick of the palsy was committed to the authority of Christ's Word, "Man, thy sins are forgiven thee." He was healed physically and spiritually. Then Matthew, a tax collector, submitted to the authority of Christ Word, "Follow me." Matthew became one of the apostles, the chosen twelve. And so, the key to overcoming those really difficult days is tied-up in the act of submitting (surrendering) oneself by faith into the hand of God for deliverance.

There are four essential biblical locks into which you may insert the *key of submission* and find help against a rogue day: The lock of keeping a joyful spirit; the lock of an understanding mind; the lock of a surrendered will; and the lock of a believing heart.

So, let's get started.

I.

The Key of Submission Into The Lock of a Joyful Attitude

The caption on the front page of the Mobile Register read: *Church Carnage in Baton Rouge*. The enraged husband, nostrils flared, one hand balled into a tight fist, the other welded around his weapon, mindless anger seething across his contorted brow in a hot sweat, entered The Ministry of Jesus Christ Church. Compelled by insane passions, he'd made his plan hours before that somebody was going to die.

When the carnage was finished, Anthony had done just that; he killed his estranged wife's grandparents, her great-aunt, a cousin, and his wife. It was all done so efficiently, so methodically. Just the way he had planned. Even Anthony was surprised that he had actually carried it out.

And what about those he killed? Did they wake up Sunday morning with a dread of doom? Did they know that only hours were left in this earthly life? Of course not, they saw the morning sun rise to a new day, a day they expected to greet with arms wide open. How could they have known that this day held such horror? That this was their rogue day?

Rogue days are devastating, rising up out of no where. They come without warning. And there you are in the bone-crushing, heart-wrenching aftermath. You are left dazed and bewildered, shocked to the core of your soul, and numbed to the center of your being. Those in the church did not even see it coming. Family and friends are left with broken pieces and the challenge to make some sense of it all.

Most people survive after long periods of dark anguish, but as expected, many do not. The emotional and spiritual suffering is too overwhelming. And somewhere in the midst of so great a trial, we are reminded just how fragile life really is.

For believers, there is help when a rogue day comes crashing over the tranquility of life. The first thing you must do is count (not to 10), but learn to count the importance of keeping *a joyful spirit*. I know how this must sound; that is, keeping joy when your heart is broken and life has lost its savor. If there is any virtue in "keeping joy" in the midst of physical, emotional, or spiritual devastation, it is this: The injunction to stay joyful in joyless circumstances comes only from the Bible, God's Word. There is ultimate authority behind this idea of using "joy" to lance the boil of rogue-day pain because God's truth is empowerment to man in his traumas of life. Indeed, we are told in the book of Nehemiah, "Neither be ye sorry; for the joy of the Lord is your strength."[1]

In the Book of James, we find this attitude of Joy-faith. The author offers the importance of keeping a joyful spirit. "Count it all joy," James wrote, "when you fall into divers (different kinds) of temptations (or trials)."[2]

Now, what is James saying? Simply and practically, we are told that, "outlook determines outcomes." Some have put it this way: "Putting some altitude in your attitude." This spiritual joy is all about allowing the Lord to develop in us a positive and proactive attitude toward the trials of life. Attempting to escape the inherent trials of life is not possible. We're not to seek trials, or pretend the enduring of trials is pleasant. Nevertheless, we are called to adopt this attitude of joy in times of adversity.

Humanly speaking, it may seem incredulous, not normal, or even a bit strange to suggest that one respond to external loss with internal joy. But before you decide to dismiss this approach to managing a rogue day, at least give this author space to explain his position. James gives us four reasons *why a joy-faith attitude is needed.*

Trials Should Be Expected

First, we are told that there is an expectancy to trials: It is not "if" they will come, but "when" they will come. The author of the Book of James, chapter 1, and verse 2, said: "My brethren, count it all joy *when* ye fall into divers temptations." God's Word alerts us to expect trials. The Lord Jesus instructed believers that, "In the world you shall have tribulations..."[3] The Apostle Paul wrote that, "We must through much tribulation enter the Kingdom of God."[4]

Paul was expressly warned to expect suffering. When the Apostle Paul encountered the glorified Jesus on the Damascus Road, Paul's life was transformed. Paul was the persecutor of the early church. After this miraculous event he became a preacher of the blessed Gospel of Jesus Christ. After this epiphany, Paul was instructed to "...go into the city..."[5] Once in Damascus, he was there for three days without sight and loss of appetite. Further instructions were given by way of a vision to a man named Ananias. He was to go to Paul and at his touch restore his sight. Paul was called to serve the Lord in a special way, and it is interesting what Jesus said: "For I will show him how great things *he must suffer* for my name's sake."[6] Paul was not told, "he might suffer," or "could suffer," but that "he must suffer..." Paul was warned of the trials that would come with putting Christ first. And indeed, Paul did suffer.

The account of the sufferings of Paul is found in 2 Corinthians 4, 6, & 12. These "sufferings" of which the Lord spoke, continued in Paul's life for thirty years.

We would pause to review a catalog of Paul's trials:

> *Evil and religious men plotted to kill him in Damascus (Acts 9:24). They did the same in Jerusalem (Acts 9:29). They drove him out of Antioch (Acts 13:50). They attempted to stone him in Iconium (Acts 14:5). And they did stone him and leave him for dead in Lystra (Acts 14:19). In Philippi they beat him with rods and put him in stocks (Acts 16:23,24). In Thessalonica the Jews and a contemptuous mob tried to mob him (Acts 17:5). They drove him out of Berea (Acts 17:13-14). They Plotted against him in*

> *Corinth (Acts 18:12). In Ephesus they almost killed him (Acts 19:29; 2 Corinthians 1:8,9). In Corinth again, shortly after he had written this Epistle, they plotted his death (Acts 20:3). In Jerusalem again they would have made a quick end to him, except for the Roman soldiers (Acts 22). Then he was imprisoned in Caesarea for two years and two more years in Rome.*

But let us not forget that there were unrecorded beatings, imprisonments, shipwrecks, continuous hardships, and privations which Paul endured.[7] In the end, this great soldier of the cross was taken to Rome and there, like his Master, was executed as a common criminal.[8]

Yes, Paul suffered. The Lord warned him it would be so and that he should expect these rogue days.

To be sure, no trial of life is pleasurable. And yet, this trusted saint, crushed and about to be poured-out, is singing his midnight hymn of praise to the Lord: "And at midnight Paul and Silas prayed, *and sang praises unto God:* and the prisoners heard them."[9]

Only "counting it all joy," and having a joy-faith attitude, could Paul have endured such rogue days of intense emotional, physical, and spiritual suffering.

The Lord Jesus predicted his rogue days: He expected trials and troubles, like rabid dogs, to attack His life. After instructing the disciples that they should tell no man that he was Jesus the Christ, he informed them of the rogue days that were ahead:

> *"From that time forth began Jesus to shew unto His disciples, how that He must go unto*

> *Jerusalem, and suffer many things of the elders
> and chief priests and scribes, and be killed,
> and be raised again the third day."[10]*

The Lord was very much aware of His own rogue days. He lived his earthly life expecting such times. And the scriptures remind us: "...*who for the joy* that was set before him endured the cross, despising the shame, and is set down at the right hand of the throne of God."[11]

As in the life of Paul and our Lord, this joy-faith is closely connected with spiritual strength, or as the author of Hebrews records, "endurance." Without this inner joy that God is in control, no matter the trials, endurance is not possible. The flesh is much too weak and spiritually anemic to confront a rogue day.[12]

Perhaps, you can manage a "really bad day," in your own strength, but a rogue day is quite another thing. A rogue day has the potential to take your life.

The Lord Jesus expected his rogue day to come. We would remember our Lord's experience in the Garden of Gethsemane. The account of this solemn event is recorded in the Gospel of Matthew: "Then cometh Jesus with them unto a place called Gethsemane..."[13] In this garden, this grove of olive trees, our Lord's soul would feel the crushing weight of the shadow of the cross and all the horrors of it. Then we are informed of the tremendous spiritual oppression he endured: "My soul," He said, "is exceedingly sorrowful, even unto death."[14] Luke's account goes even further, telling us that His soul was under such stress that an angel was dispatched to strengthen Him: "And being in an agony he prayed the more earnestly: And His sweat was as it were great drops of blood falling down to the ground."[15]

Though the scriptures do not tell us what the Lord Jesus endured in that dark night of Gethsemane's Garden, we can speculate with some assurance that he foresaw the horror of this rogue day approaching. He saw the brutality of his scourging and the horror of his own crucifixion.

Unlike you and me, because of his sinless nature, the Lord Jesus vicariously felt his death before it actually happened. He felt the cruel Roman soldier's flogging with the whip of braided leather thongs of iron balls and bone chips. He felt it strike his flesh causing deep bruises, contusions, and lacerations. From the top of his shoulders, to the buttocks, to the back of his legs, the Lord Jesus felt the tearing of his flesh into quivering ribbons of bleeding skin. He felt his veins laid bare, His muscles exposed, and his back so shredded that parts of his spine protruded. The beating was so horrible and brutal that our Lord would, in one doctor's estimation, have suffered hypovolemic shock which means low blood pressure.[16] This is why we are told in Matthew, that the Lord Jesus finally collapsed and that one Simon of Cyrene was ordered to carry the cross.[17] The blood loss was sufficient that it caused strength to leave the body of the Lord Jesus. He felt the brutality and horror of the scourging he must bare, and that is why he prayed: "O Father, if it be possible, let this cup pass from me: Nevertheless not as I will, but as Thou wilt."[18]

Before the 7-inch spikes were driven into his hands and feet, He was already in critical condition and quite aware what awaited him. His death was eminent. And His was the most horrendous and celebrated rogue day of all, the infamous day of the death of God.

You asked, "What was he thinking?"

He was thinking of you and me, because the scriptures say: "Surely, He hath borne our griefs...carried our sorrows...was wounded for our transgressions...bruised for our iniquities...and the chastisement of our peace was upon Him and with His stripes we are healed."[19]

He saw his rogue day coming. It had been predicted by the Old Testament prophets. He accepted and voluntarily chose to suffer and die. It was his mission, His destiny. He was born to this end, to be the Redeemer of mankind. And as we said earlier, this expectation was met with joy.[20]

Believers would do well to understand that we are not exempt from rogue days. Paul reminded that we too will suffer. He said: "For unto you it is given in the behalf of Christ, not only to believe on Him, but also to suffer for His sake."[21] From Paul's standpoint of personal experience, he was well qualified to write and say, "to you it hath been granted on behalf of Christ...to suffer." In the midst of our trials, we must not forget that the suffering the child of God endures is only short-term. The Bible encourages us, saying, "But the God of all Grace, who hath called us unto his eternal glory by Christ Jesus, *after that ye have suffered a while*, make you perfect, stablish, strengthen, and settle you."[22]

Where did the idea come that Christians are trial-free? Nothing could be further from the truth. In this life "really bad days" and "Rogue days" are woven into the fabric of earthly life. Every day, somewhere, someone suffers. Everyone has trials. All are subject to the frailties and harsh realities of living in a rogue world. All humanity is subject to the trials of life. But the difference between unbelievers vs. believers is that believers are not alone in the valley of the shadow of death. With joy, they trust the unseen hand of God to direct their steps and assure their outcome. Mature believers have been warned. And we are to expect that sooner or later, our own rogue day will come. And when it arrives, God will help us to respond in joy; a joy which keeps trusting the Lord and reminds us that we are not alone.

Scattered People

In the Book of James we are informed to whom this letter is written: "...to the twelve tribes which are scattered abroad..."[23] This was written to the twelve tribes scattered, or phraseology that leads one to believe that James is referring to spiritual Israel. Spiritual Israel would be a reference to Christians whether they are Jew or Gentile. To the early believers who had so much trouble with orthodox Jews and Jewish religious leaders, it should not be surprising that Christians viewed themselves as the true Israel.

Paul addressed this description of the Christian Church. He said: "Who are Israelites? To whom pertaineth the adoption...?"[24] Then Paul said: "...For they are not all Israel, which are Israel."[25] And finally he said:

> *"Neither, because they are the seed of Abraham, are they all children: but, in Isaac shall they seed be called. That is, they which are the children of the flesh, these are not the children of God: but the children of the promise are counted for the seed."*[26]

The children of promise after the flesh, of course, would be Israel. But in the spiritual sense, the promise of becoming a child of God belongs to those, as Jesus said, "You must be born again."[27] Those trusting Christ for salvation constitute the spiritual Israel, whether they are Jew or Gentile.

Christians are God's scattered people. Before our Lord's ascension, he defined us scattered people when he said: "... and ye will be witnesses unto me in both in Jerusalem, and in all Judea, and in Samaria, and unto the utter most parts of the world."[28] Believers are called "scattered" because the world in which we live continues to need the scattered seed, the sowing of God's Word. Sometimes we forget that the devil is well and alive on planet earth doing his work of severing, separating, scattering.

God's scattered people live in a divided world and we must be aware that the culprit behind our trials is the devil. Believers have an adversary who seeks to abort God's will that believers are his witnesses.[29] "Be sober, be vigilant," Peter wrote, "because your adversary the devil, as a roaring lion, walketh about seeking whom he may devour."[30]

If we compare 1 John 2:16, with Genesis 3:6, we will learn that the devil does indeed work to undo God's will in the believer's life. The devil has three entrances into our lives:

> *"For all that is in the world, the lust of the flesh, and the lust of the eyes, and the pride of life, is not of the Father, but is of the world."*[31]

The lust of the flesh speaks of the graving for sensual gratification. The lust of the eyes addresses the stimulation of ungodly longing of the mind. And the pride of life is to act like little gods. And John said that these worldly corridors into our lives, "...is not of the Father, but is of the world."

When the first man and woman closed the door to intimate fellowship with God, Satan was able to open these dark doors into the human soul. Through these corridors, if you will, the devil comes to us and influences us toward evil. You essentially find that the devil used these corridors to reach Eve, and then Adam:

> *"For God doth know that in the day ye eat thereof, then your eyes shall be opened, and ye shall be as gods, knowing good and evil. And when the woman saw that the tree was good for food, and that it was pleasant to the eyes, and a tree to be desired to make one wise, she took of the fruit thereof, and did eat, and gave also unto her husband with her; and he did eat."*[32]

Notice that these same three doors are identified in 1John 2:16:

> *Lust of the flesh, "...she took and did eat..."*
>
> *Lust of the eyes, "...the woman saw...it was pleasant to the eyes..."*
>
> *Pride of life, "...ye shall be as gods..."*

The devil is able to use these three axises of evil to influence our hearts and minds against the Lord. This is the kind of limited power he welds in our lives. So, be warned that the devil is allowed a limited power to influence the nations and peoples of the world. Some may believe that this dark creature is all power and wisdom, but such is not the case. Yet, it would be a mistake to underestimate what power and wisdom the devil does wield. Limited power is granted to the devil, he is able to touch our flesh with disease and suffering.[33] But the power of life and death is not within his authority. Only God is the "Giver" and the "Taker" of life.

Apparently, the devil has access before the throne of God and is able to present himself before the Lord with the sons of God.[34] In one of these meeting, God dropped the name of Job: "Have you considered my servant Job what a fine man he is?"[35] And immediately, the devil challenged Job's character and God allowed the devil to test Job. But the truth we need to glean is found when God said to the devil, "...he is in thine hand; but save his life."[36] In other words, you have the power to touch his flesh, but it is not in your power to take his life. The devil has a limited power, power that must meet the approval of God. The devil could do nothing to Job until God allowed it.

Again, this joy is the assurance that we are not alone and that God is indeed "Emmanuel——God with us." Nothing can happen in the believer's life outside the permissive will of God. And let us not forget that we live in an evil world where bad things happen to bad people, good people, and yes, even to God's people. Things happen, but that does not mean that we are alone, forgotten, and out of the control of the Lord.

Sickness will come.

Accidents will happen.

Disappointments will occur.

Tragedies will assault you.

Misfortune will come knocking.

Death will stalk you. But through it all, we have the promise that the Lord will give us grace and strength to endure.[37] The Lord will not leave us without hope.

The world is still an evil place filled with mishaps and potholes of disaster. That is why The Bible warns that life is fragile. "Life is a vapor," we are taught, "that appeareth for a little time, and then vanisheth away."[38]

So, Peter reminded us of being scattered people and of the trials that will challenge and confront every believer. He said: "Beloved, think it not strange concerning the fiery trials which is to try you, as though some strange thing happened to you."[39]

There is this second reason we must learn to manage the trials of life: Don't forget that we are scattered people. You have not entered heaven, yet. The devil is still well and active on planet earth doing his work of dividing, separating, scattering. His strategy has always been to divide and conquer.

Joy Robbers

We need this joy-faith attitude in the trials of life, because trials are designed to rob you of your joy in Christ. It is not "if" trials will come, but "when." And so, the child of God must anticipate, or learn to count, that any day may emerge as a rogue day. And readiness of joy-faith is critical when these horrific events suddenly explode and impact our lives to the very core.

Two days ago, a young man in our church was coming home from work in the early morning hours. He fell asleep at the wheel and drifted to the curb where he hit the rear of a garbage truck. It was a terrible collision, his knees were broken, his hip removed from its socket, and serious head traumas. The young man was saved only by the grace of Almighty God. As I visited in the hospital, I was struck by the serene stillness of his mother's spirit as she calmly spoke to me saying, "God saved my son. I could be at the funeral home, but I'm here with my son who is alive. And I thank the Lord for sparing my boy." Hers was a readiness of joy-faith that met the hour of a rogue event.

In James 1:2, the word "fall into" means to "encounter, or come across." This same word "to fall" is used in the Parable of the Good Samaritan, who "fell into, or encountered," thieves and robbers. We are told:

> *"A certain man went down from Jerusalem to Jericho, and fell among thieves, which stripped him of his raiment, and wounded him, and departed, leaving him half dead."*[40]

This man had no name. He is a certain man. When he awoke, anticipating a pleasant day of travel, he had no idea how this twenty-mile journey from Jerusalem to Jericho would unfold. Little did "certain man" know, that this was to be his rogue day, a day where he would be left stripped, wounded, and half dead. As this story tells us, "A certain man went *down*..." Indeed, this was to be his "down-day." He had not paused at the beginning of this day's journey to count the unexpected. And yet, the life he lived was the same we live today, days designed to unexpectedly rob us of the joy of living, and even life itself.

The phone on my desk rang, even as I penned the words above. A certain man, to whom I will minister, has just been told the cancer had spread. The news will not be received well, as one would expect. It is a rogue day, a day of unexpected fear, anguish, and doubt. And how will this *certain man* approach this trial of disease? We must learn to anticipate the unexpected and as James said, "...count it all joy..." Let the Presence of the Lord to be our strength and our joy.

Only Christ will not forsake us. He is the Good Samaritan who will see to our afflictions; come to us with compassion; bind our wounds; bring healing to our souls; direct our paths to safety; show mercy and everlasting kindness. In Him we receive this attitude of joy that gives us the power to overcome a rogue day.

But life is a wonder, a joy to experience, a beautiful journey full of excitement, inspiration, and joy unspeakable. And yet, life is an all-to-short and fragile event.

The duration of Life is like that of a Mayfly on a warm June morning. Five minutes of life is all nature has allotted this curious insect. In five minutes, the female Mayfly must emerge from a year's hibernation at the bottom of a lake, rise to the surface, find a mate, journey back down to the bottom of that lake, lay her eggs, and then die. It's interesting, but the scientific name of the mayfly is Ephemeropetla, meaning, "short-lived-flyer."

In the total scheme of things, human life is really so short-lived. As people often say, "the water passes ever so swiftly under the bridge of life." And it does: One minute you are young, energetic, and full of hopes and dreams; then in the next, you are caught wondering where all that time has gone. The scriptures would concur that life is short:

> *"Whereas ye know not what shall be on the morrow. For what is your life? Is it even a vapor, that appeareth for a little time, and then vanisheth away."*[41]

Or, in The Book of Job, where we are told:

> *"My days are swifter than a weaver's shuttle and are spent without hope...*[42] *Now my days are swifter than a post: they flee away, they see no good.*[43] *"...Man that is born of a woman is of few days, and full of troubles. He cometh forth like a flower, and is cut down: He fleeth also as a shadow, and continueth not."*[44]

Or, hear the Psalmist say:

> *"Behold, thou has made my days as an hand breath; and mine age is as nothing before Thee..."*[45]

Or, listen to Peter's words:

> *"For all flesh is as grass, and all the glory of man as the flower of grass. The grass withereth, and the flower thereof falleth away."*[46]

Life is transient. Life's duration is really much like the humble Mayfly: Short-lived-flyers are we all.

In Stephen Cherniske's book, "The Metabolic Plan," he makes an arresting statement:

> *"An amazing thing happens as we grow older. I'm not talking about the appearance of gray hair, expanding waistlines, and a sudden fondness for La-Z-Boy furniture. Far more amazing is the shift in our perceptions and priorities. One day, we are happily oblivious to our mortality, and then wham, we turn forty and suddenly realize that the fun and games do not go on forever. Then, and this is even more dramatic, we turn fifty and double wham, we're gripped by the sense that:*
>
> *1. Our life in more than half over.*
>
> *2. The half that's over was the fun part.*
>
> *3. The rest will include progressive disability, degeneration, and decrepitude, in other words, pain and suffering."*[47]

Somewhere along the path of life, this journey down from Jerusalem to Jericho, a reasonable, thinking man must grapple with his own mortality. Murphy's Law is always in play: "Anything that can go wrong, will go wrong." We must be prepared in our walk with the Lord to handle anything, any rogue day that suddenly rises-up, trusting him for the strength and the joy of His Presence. Has he not said, "In the world ye shall have trials and tribulations, but be of good cheer: *I have overcome the world.*"[48]

Faulty Priorities

We need a Joy-faith attitude, one that is Christ-centered, because all too often our estimation of what is important in life is faulty. Our priorities are out-of-whack. James said, "...count it..."[49] The word *count* is a financial term and means "to evaluate." In other words, our values in life determine our evaluations of life. If one counts comfort, material things, worldly pleasures, or even family and friends as the more important things in life, it will not be possible to overcome a rogue day. We need a much stronger anchor than the latter affections can offer.

So, what is this anchor, this strong mask on a tempest tossed? If you will *count* Jesus Christ (that is, to reckon him as Lord and Savior and evaluate him as your source of impregnable strength...your anchor) then when the trials come, you will experience the joy of the Presence of the Lord.

How is that possible?

It is possible because in him you are never alone. In your darkest hour, even as you walk through the valley of the shadow of death, he is there to strengthen and direct your way. He is Emmanuel, "God with us."[50] Has He not said, "...I will never leave thee, or forsake thee?"[51] For those who trust The Lord, there is the promise of His divine presence and constancy. You don't have to walk alone through life's perilous way. He says to us: "...I am with thee, and will keep thee in all places whither thou goeth..."[52] When you need help for your weary soul, The Lord offers rest: "My presence will go with thee, and I will give thee rest."[53]

The Apostle Paul is one of our prime examples of the Christo-Centric Principle and reliance on the strength of Joy-faith. When you study the life of this great man of faith, you soon come to realize that only Christ mattered. He evaluated everything in life out of his personal experience with Jesus Christ. Paul gave us his accounting of life. He said:

> *"I count all things but loss for the excellency of the knowledge of Christ Jesus: For whom I suffered the loss of all things, and do count them but dung, that I may win Christ."*[54]

For Paul, in spite of his trials, only Christ counted. And he evaluated every thing else in life from his own personal experience with the Lord Jesus. For Paul, to win Christ meant personally experiencing the Presence of the power of Christ in this life. But to win Christ also gave Paul the assurance of a glorious future.

If we live only for the present and forget the future, the trials of life can make us bitter. So, let us *count* Christ as the most important influence in our lives. And let us reckon that every day the future is coming to us, not only with the expected trials of life which challenge and test us, but also the unexpected trial of a rogue day. And let us be mindful that we have a Champion in the arena, a Captain in the storms of life. And in him we will find the peace and the power of his joy to overcome all obstacles.

A man and his wife once visited a world-famous weaver and watched as he worked the loom. They noticed that the underside of the rug was not very beautiful: The pattern was obscure and the loose ends of yarn dangled. The man at the loom commented to the couple: "Please, dear friends, don't judge the worker or his work by looking at the wrong side."

In the same way, we are presently looking at life on the wrong side of God's tapestry; the loose ends are the trials of life and they are not very pretty. Only the ONE, sitting busily at the divine loom of life sees the finished pattern. So we must not judge him or his work from our limited vantage point. When all is finished, then we will know the completed design of the mystery of God.

The first key to overcoming a rogue day is the key of Joy-Faith. In simple, childlike faith, claim the joy of the Presence of Christ in the advent of your rogue day. Choose to let his joy, be your joy: "These things have I spoken unto you, that *my joy* might remain in you and that your joy might be full."[55]

Why is this joy-Spirit critical in the life of the believer? Joy is critical in the life of the believer because trials are expected: Believers are a scattered people. There is the threat of Joy robbers, and faulty priorities in life.

The end

2

The Second Key:
An Understanding Mind

There are several possible attitudes you can take toward the hardships of life: You can rebel by adopting a spirit of defiance which declares loud and clear for all to hear that you don't need God, or anyone else in your time of distress.[1] You say, "I'll fight my own way out." Or, you can lose heart (a fainting spirit) and you say, "I can't take this any more. I'm going to end my life."[2]

As I penned these words, one of the workers in our Day Care School received a phone call that a cousin in Louisiana, and I quote, "Blew his brains out." He was going through a divorce. How tragic and senseless. We would be shocked how many burdened people turn to suicide as a way to deal with their rogue day. I trust his soul was prepared to meet The Lord. Some will grumble and complain about their troubles.[3] Or, you can indulge in self-pity and say, "Why me, Lord?"[4] By the way, why not you? What makes you think you are any different from the rest of us?

On the other end of the line was the quaking voice of Dennis Barnes. "Brother Paul," he said, "my son Delmar just received the results from his tests. The doctor told him that he had tumors in some of his limp nodes and on his saliva gland."

"Dennis," I said, "I'm so sorry to hear about this."

"Yeah, I am too." Over the receiver there was the sound of lungs expanding, then the release of slow breath. "He's so young you know. And he's got kids, a wife...you know how it is."

"How's he taking the news?"

"I tried to call," said Dennis, "but he won't talk. His wife said he just got in his truck and drove off. He told her he needed to be alone and do some thinking."

Trials come to all sooner, or later. Rogue days are not age-sensitive. Again, it's not "if," but "when." It's just the kind of world in which we live, a world of trials and tribulations.[5] We just need to be prepared when our time comes.

All of the above are options, but none offer enduring moral strength. Delmar chose the "why me?" option. The cousin in Louisiana chose "I'm going to end my life" option. This is not criticism. It is simply an observation of how we attempt to deal with our own rogue days. But the best way to handle a rogue event is with an understanding mind. When you ask the question, "why me?" understand that God does not arbitrarily decide to zap people with sickness, or any other trial of life. But when sickness and trials come, God will use them to perfect our relationship with him.

Maybe that's why the author of James said, "...count it all joy when you fall..." Nothing is more important than one's relationship with the Lord. The Lord knows that too many times we must endure a rogue day before we understand the importance of seeking the face of God.

It has been observed that God is trying to produce Christ-likeness in each of his children and that the process necessarily requires suffering, frustration, and perplexity. It is not that God targets you and me for pain and sorrow. No, nothing could be farther from the truth. The Lord loves us and is not willing that any should travail or perish. Yet, God works with what we have given him: A world lost in sin and alienated from his friendship. Did he not warn the federated head of the human race that there would be dire consequences if he disobeyed the command to eat of the forbidden fruit? Indeed, God told the first man, Adam; that *he would surely die* if he ate from the tree of the Knowledge of Good and Evil.[6]

Encompassed in this word "die" is the source of humanity's corruption, frailty, and destruction. Man chose to disobey God and the result was alienation between God and man. This alienation resulted in the aberrations of War, man's inhumanities to his brother, violence, self-destruction, disease, heartache of a million tears, sorrow, anguish, separation from his Creator, and finally death itself. These aberrations come from the same fountain head: That unfortunate choice to disobey God. In fact, think about this: If it was not for the grace and the goodness of God, death would immediately consume you and me. But in the wisdom of God, He so designed our bodies that they replenish themselves every day by discarding and renewing the body by some three-hundred billion cells.[7] Next time you blame God for being the "bad guy" think about his matchless mercy and love. If God did not love the sinner, the human race would have self-destructed and never moved passed Adam and Eve. It is a miracle of love and grace, wouldn't you say, that humanity has made its way thus far?

It was around the middle of April, 2006, when my third son, Michael, asked me if he could plant a small garden in the backyard. When he was in high school, he and his friend Ryan took a class in horticulture. So, I said okay… why not? As I expected, Michael made a Grade-A, number one mess throughout the garage to grow his victory garden. But what did that matter, I've been housing, Willard, his 50-pound retriever for the last year. Anyway, it is now the beginning of June, and the garden is a beautiful sight of hairy-corn, yellow squash, red tomatoes, and green peppers. I've got to hand it to the boys, despite the mess, they put a lot of work into that garden; especially, since the last few months offered very little, if any rain. Every day they had to water the garden.

The point here is this: The fruit of the spirit cannot be produced when all is sunshine, there must be storm clouds filled with life-giving rain. Trials never seem pleasant, but The Bible reminds us that afterwards they yield the peaceable fruit of righteousness. This observation is correct and thoroughly biblical. The author of Hebrews tells us:

> *"Now no chastening for the present seemeth to be joyous, but grievous: nevertheless afterwards it yields the peaceable fruit of righteousness unto them which are exercised thereby."*[8]

Charles Kettering, noted industrialist, was reported to have said: "Problems are the price of progress. Don't bring me anything but problems. Good news weakens me."

And so the question arises: How is it possible to rejoice when my rogue day comes? The second key that unlocks the joy of the Lord is *an understanding mind*. The author of James said, "Knowing this..."[9]

The key word is "Knowing." It means to have an understanding mind that is capable of realizing why trials come. So what is it that we should know about trials?

In a rogue day event, an understanding mind will know three things: Faith is always tested, such testing works for you and not against you, and spiritual maturity is forged in the fire of our trials.

Tested Faith

For Heaven's approval, faith in Christ must be spiritually tested. It becomes clear as you study the Bible that God will allow the testing of our faith to bring out our best for him. In the Book of James our author spoke of "...the trying (testing) of your faith..."[10] How will the Lord test our faith?

He may demand great sacrifice. Abraham was tested. We are told: "And it came to pass after these things, that God did tempt (test) Abraham, and said unto him, Abraham: and he said, Behold, here am I. And he said, Take now thy son, thine only son Isaac, whom thou loveth, and get thee into the land of Moriah; and offer him there for a burnt offering upon one of the mountains which I shall tell thee of."[11]

He may lead into a difficult way. In the Book of Deuteronomy, we see how The Lord will direct his people by the hard way. We are told: "And thou shalt remember all the way which The Lord thy God led thee forty years in the wilderness, to humble thee, and to prove (test) thee, to know what was in thine heart, whether thou wouldest keep his commandments, or no."[12]

He may give opportunities for choice. In the Book of 1 Kings, we see that The Lord may place before us the freedom to choose. We are told: "In Gibeon the Lord appeared to Solomon in a dream by night: And God said, "what I shall give thee."[13] The Psalmist said, "...for the righteous God trieth the hearts and reins."[14]

He may propose hard tasks. In the Gospel of John, the Lord may test our faith by insisting we do something that humanly speaking seems impossible. We are told: "When Jesus then lifted up his eyes, and saw a great company come unto him, He saith unto Philip, Whence shall we buy bread, that these may eat? And this he said to prove (test) him: For he knew what He would do."[15] And let's not forget when The Lord delayed his response time to Martha and Mary that their faith might be tested in his ability to do the impossible. We are told that "when he heard therefore that he (Lazarus) was sick, He abode two days still in the same place where he was."[16]

This would be a good place to bring up the principle of "God Room." The "God Room" lesson helps us to understand why the Lord test faith: He wants you and me to trust Him for the impossible…to rise above our own human abilities...to accomplish hard tasks. "God Room," according to Bob Pierce, past president of World Vision, is this:

> *"'God Room' is when you see a need and it's bigger than your human abilities to meet it. But you accept the challenge. You trust God to bring in the finances and the materials to meet that need."18 Nothing is a miracle until it reaches the area where the utmost that human effort can do still isn't enough. God has to fill that space——that room——between what's possible and what he wants done that's impossible. That's what I mean by 'God Room.'"[17]*

Ken Monroe called yesterday. Said he needed to talk. I said fine, I'll be in my office. Come on down. Fifteen minutes later Ken was sitting across the desk visibly distraught, eyes swollen, tears running down both sides of his cheeks. For years Ken had been trying to get-along with an in-law who was determined to be hateful and full of spite. To make matters worst, both men were brothers in the Lord. It was a sad situation, one that on this particular day had finally come to a head. The festering hostility between the two had come dangerously close to exchanging physical blows. And so here sat Ken...heartbroken, no peace, no joy, and an unwanted bitter spirit. An otherwise gentle and kind man, Ken was suffering from "spiritual oppression."

What is "spiritual oppression?" Spiritual oppression is a satanic assault against a believer with the objective of stealing his/her joy and crippling their walk with the Lord. The

Lord warned Peter concerning such oppression: "Simon, Simon, behold

Satan hath desired to have you, that he may sift you as wheat. But I have prayed for thee, that thy faith fail not..."[18]

Ken had been trying through his own efforts and abilities to deal with an ever increasing volatile situation, but the task was impossible. Little did Ken know, he was being sifted, sifted to the point where he was doubting his own salvation.

Now, all this to say: Can any good come out of spiritual oppression? Spiritual oppression will drive you to your knees before the Lord and cause you to finally admit, "Lord, I can't handle this in my strength any longer, I'm too weak. I need you to restore me and intercede on my behalf."

In the two hours that Ken & I talked, we learned something only discovered in the trials of life. We learned that in a hard task, a difficult conflict of life, God takes the advantage to *test our faith*. As the Lord said to Peter, "that he had prayed for him that his faith fail not," so it was that these prayers stayed a hostile spirit from exchanging blows. Ken was whipped-down, but he was not wiped-out. No, his Lord helped him to overcome this oppression. Yes, Ken's faith had been tested and found wanting. But as he left my office that same faith was stronger and now able to deal productively with the issue before him. Why was Ken's faith stronger? It was stronger because Ken finally got out of the way and let God have room to work. That is the "God Room" principle.

When we've done all that's humanly possible, then step out of the way and allow the Lord to do the impossible. As Moses said when he started to lead the Lord's people across the Red Sea: "Fear not, stand still, and see the salvation of the Lord, which He will show you today: for the Egyptians whom you have seen today, ye shall see them again no more forever."[19]

He may allow us to suffer as we serve him. We are reminded: "For unto you it is given in behalf of Christ, not only to believe on Him, but also to suffer for His sake."[20] We remember Paul and Silas: "And when they had laid many stripes upon them, they cast them into prison, charging the jailer to keep them safely. Who, receiving such a charge, thrust them into the inner prison, and made their feet fast in the stocks."[21]

He may allow temptation. Spiritual warfare is real in the believer's life. We must be able to recognize the enemy's attack if we will be good soldiers of the cross. "My brethren," James said, "count it all joy when ye fall into divers temptations; knowing this, that the trying of your faith worketh patience."[22]

What areas of your life have been tested recently? How did you respond? As you went through your trials, did you stop to consider if God was testing your faith?

God tested his own Son. He allowed the devil to tempt Jesus: "Then was Jesus led," we are told, "up of the Spirit into the wilderness to be *tempted* (tested) of the devil."[23] So, why would you think it a strange thing that the Lord would test your faith?

You say, "I don't understand. Why does God allow trials into my life?" God allows trials in our lives because he wants our faith to grow and be strong. God wants us to be like His Son, Jesus, of whom it is written: "Though He were a Son, yet learned he obedience by the things which He suffered; and being made perfect, He became the author of eternal salvation unto all them that obey him."[24]

A young man was trying to establish himself as a peach grower. He had worked hard and invested all he had in a peach orchard that blossomed wonderfully. Then the frost came. He did not go to church the next Sunday. Finally, the preacher went to see him to find out why he was missing church.

"I'm not going to church anymore," said the young man. "Do you think I can worship a God who cares so little that He would let a frost kill all my peaches?"

The old minister looked at him for a few moments in silence, and then said kindly: "God loves you better than he does your peaches. He knows that while peaches do better without frost, it's impossible to grow the best men without frost. His object is to grow men not peaches."

Do you want to grow in your faith and experience joy in your trials? Then have an understanding mind: God will test your faith.

For You, Not Against You

Someone has said, "What doesn't kill you makes you stronger." In the Christian life trials are not meant to kill us, they are meant to strengthen our spiritual life and draw us nearer to the Lord. There very well may be something to the adage weight lifters like to throw around: "No pain, no gain."

As a college student, I decided to lift weights. The next day my body was stiff and sore. The coach passed me in the hall and I told him that weight-lifting wasn't making me any muscles; it was just making me sore. I'll never forget his response. He said, "You are one of the ones who will never know."

Trials, in a sense, are the weights that exercise and strengthen the spirit of man. The coach is The Holy Spirit of God. The weight of our trials need not crush the life out of our souls, if only we will discipline ourselves and trust in the guidance and inspiration of our heavenly coach. You say, "But trials hurt." Or, "I don't believe they will strengthen me." And as an old mentor once said to me, I say to you: "You are one of the ones who will never know."

This word "trying" can also mean "approval." It presents our faith as a precious metal, a metal like gold, which is being tested by God to see if it is genuine and stress-proof. Scripture informs us:

> *"That the trial of your faith, being much more precious than gold that perishes, though it be tried with fire' might be found unto praise and honor and glory at the appearing of Jesus Christ."*[25]

In this sense trials can work for us, not against us. In the wisdom of God our trials become like a refining fire in the hands of the Lord. Even rogue days have a purpose to perform. We are told: "For our light affliction which is but for a moment, worketh for us a far more exceeding and eternal weight of glory."[26]

Our faith toward the Lord can be likened as a raw ore sample and God as the Master Goldsmith. Our raw faith must pass through the divine smelting process to separate the impurities. It has been told when a Goldsmith smelts ore in a superheated furnace that the way he can tell the gold is pure, is when he can see his image in the liquid gold. When God can see the image of his beloved Son, the Lord Jesus in your life, he knows the quality of your faith is maturing. So, if you want to grow in your faith and have joy in trials, understand that trials represent the furnace fires of this life. In this sense, trials will work for you, not against you.

Toward a Mature Faith

We are not left in doubt what God wants to produce in our lives. He wants to produce patience. This word for patience means to endure, to be steadfast, to persevere. Patience is needed to develop spiritual stamina. A tested faith becomes a stronger faith because patience keeps the believer going when times are rough and days are difficult. These enviable traits of endurance, steadfastness, and perseverance help us to wait on the Lord. And waiting patiently on the Lord helps us to mature in our walk with God. The Bible reminds us:

> *"...but we glory in tribulations also: Knowing that tribulation worketh patience; and patience experience; and experience hope."*[27]

People begin their walk with God and here come the trials. They say, "Why is God doing this to me?" And after awhile, they quit the Lord. Why? They quit God because theirs is a lack of spiritual maturity. No patience.

How is it possible that one begins the Christian life, but later forsakes Jesus Christ? They failed to apply themselves to the study of God's Word and attain an understanding mind. They never knew that God test faith to bring out our best to his glory. They never understood that God uses the trials of life to work for us and not against us. And they never understood that trials help us to mature and build stay-power into our walk with the Lord. And yet the scriptures teach: "Knowing that tribulation worketh patience."[28]

Today I spoke to a distraught man who carried the weight of a crushed heart. His wife of many years confessed she had been unfaithful and no longer loved him. She wanted a divorce. The emotional pain was overwhelming. He had no clue she was so unhappy. Through swollen, red-glazed eyes he shared with me the agony of betrayal. The question of how she, the love of his life, could hurt him so deeply, so merciless, was like a dagger plunged to the depths of his soul.

Such pain cannot be calculated. It is too devastating, too painful; too enormous to be weighed. As he searched for an answer one thing arrested me. He said they were both Christians as if the status of being Christian should bring some immunity to bad behavior. Labeling one "Christian" apart from a serious application of the truth of God's Word is much like an otherwise useful tire that has gone flat. For a tire to work it needs a suitable amount of air pressure and frequent examination with an air gauge if it is to perform properly. Likewise, to be "Christian" calls for an understanding mind of God's Word.[29] application of God truth is mandatory.[30] It will take constant vigilance and self-examination by the scrutiny of holy scripture if we are to perform properly in the sight of God.[31]

Could this couple have averted this lapse of moral degradation had they secured for themselves the underpinning of an understanding mind in God's Word? I have the confidence to say "yes." The sad fact of being human is that we don't have to be taught to do wrong, it comes to us naturally. We are born with the proclivity of saying, "no" to God. It comes easy. The flip side of being human, however, means that we have to be taught to be godly and this behavioral quality comes to us "supernaturally." We must be trained to have an understanding mind in the things of God and the Bible is our only reliable source.

There is the story of the little girl who made herself a ruler. When dad came home from work, she said to him: "Look daddy! I'm ten foot tall." Puzzled, the dad asked, "How did you arrive at that calculation?" With scissor in her hand, the little girl proudly announced, "I made my own ruler."

People without God scorn absolute truth, particularly spiritual truth. Like this little child, they prefer to be their own judge determining what is right or wrong. No one can blame a child for thinking like a child, but an adult who wants to play god is foolish and dangerous; foolish because they make their own ruler and code of ethics; and dangerous because they expect others to dance to their warped piping. Such misguided souls would soon argue that "up is not up" and "down is not down" than acknowledge there is God; the God who is the source of all knowledge and ethical structure. It is no small wonder that The Ten Commandments is a contentious issue in American culture. In the liberal America of this present generation, a ruler has been forged. And the new motto is not "In God We Trust," but "In Man We Trust." And they chant, "Let the new world order begin."

The day of ruination for America happened when the Supreme Court took their ruler of flesh and judged the unborn fruit of the womb as non-life. Beyond human sensitivities "Roe vs. Wade" made it law to kill the most innocent creatures known to man, babies. No matter what pinnacles of achievement our nation may attain, the Sword of Damocles swings tirelessly waiting for the moment of God's righteous execution. Let there be no doubt that the hand of God is against this great nation if only for one sin, the sin of killing God's inheritance. Nothing short of a revival of repentance, burning across this land in the hearts of the people can save us now. The storehouse of God's great mercy and forgiveness is all that stands before us and ruination. Though there are other dreadful and ungodly issues, the legalizing of abortion is the most damaging sin; the repercussions we have yet to see upon our nation.

But here is the point: Without God's Divine Instruction Book, we are left to our own standards of righteousness. But the question is——who are you to define this standard, whether for yourself or others? Are you as superior in wisdom, justice, and righteousness as God himself that you should offer an alternate code of morality? And why would you embark on so futile an effort when such effective codes already exist? And yet, so many are like the little girl who told her daddy that she was ten feet tall. Is it not a fact of human nature that when Satan said to Eve, "...ye shall be as gods..." that is exactly what occurred to mankind.[32] We are born with a little god complex and we each do what we think is right according to our standards.[33]

King David made his own rules. He fell in love with another man's wife, Bathsheba. He no doubt felt as a king (a little god) that he could do anything he so desired. In short order Bathsheba conceived David's child while Uriah, her husband, was away at war. To cover-up his sin, David gave orders for Uriah to be killed on the front line. Did David's standard of righteousness work for him, obviously not. That one decision to step past the parameters of God's moral code would curse the rest of his days. And God said:

> *"Now therefore the sword shall never depart from thine house; because thou hast despised me, and hath taken the wife of Uriah the Hittite to be thy wife. Thus saith the Lord, behold, I will raise up evil against thee out of thine own house, and I will take thy wives before thine eyes, and give them unto thy neighbor, and he shall lie with thy wives in the sight of this sun. For thou didst it secretly: but I will do this thing before all Israel, and before the sun."*[34]

What did David's code of behavior do for him? "And David said to Nathan, I have sinned against the Lord."[35]

If joy will come in the midst of our rogue days, an understanding mind is an essential key that unlocks the power of joy-faith. You will come to understand that working faith will always be tested; such testing works for you, not against you, and that spiritual maturity is forged in the fire of our trials.

The end

3

The Third Key: A Surrendered Will

It was dark. The hiker hurried along the side of the road hoping to see lights just up ahead. But as fate would have it, he ventured to close to the shoulder. He slipped and fell over a cliff. Luckily, he managed to grab hold of a small tree root and stop his fall. His feet dangled beneath him and there was nothing but blackness below. He shouted: "Is anybody there?"

"Yes," replied a loud voice. "I am down here. Let yourself go. You can trust me. I am God." There was a long silence and then the hiker shouted: "Is anybody else down there?"

If the trials of our lives will have any meaning or purpose, then we must consider them as part of God's will. The thought process goes like this: We are His children,

He is our Father; therefore, whatever comes into my life my Heavenly Father must first approve it; and if my Heavenly Father approves and permits suffering to enter my life, then I will trust him and endure the cross which he has designed for me to bear; and in the process will give him glory and praise, because I know, He does all things well. As believers, we can trust that the Lord is at work perfecting our faith and relationship with him.

It is said of Jesus that "who for the *joy* that was set before him *endured* the cross, despising the shame..."[1] Our Lord, we are told, could with "joy," endure the trial of the cross. How was that possible? Joy and endurance was possible, because his was a *surrendered will* to his Heavenly Father. In sweet surrender, our Lord's suffering had purpose: The cross was his way back home to Heaven, but his suffering and subsequent death was also our way home. Did He not say to Peter and the disciples, "Whither I go, thou canst not follow me now; but thou shalt follow me afterwards?"[2] Indeed, He did. His suffering and the trial of the cross had purpose. That is why he could pray in the sorrow of a rogue event, "O, My Father, if this cup may not pass away from me, except I drink it, thy will be done."[3]

The Lord Jesus was perfectly surrendered to doing the will of His Father. He was absolutely committed and nothing could detour him. "My meat is do the will of him that sent me," Jesus said to his disciples, "and to finish his work."[4] Furthermore, Jesus made it clear that He had entered the material realm of mankind in obedience to His Father. He said:

> "For I came down from Heaven, not to do mine own will, but the will of him that sent me. And this is the Father's will which hath

> *sent me, that of all which he hath given me I should lose nothing, but should raise it up again at the last day. And this is the will of him that sent me, that ever one which seeth the Son, and believeth on him, may have everlasting life: And I will raise him up at the last day."*[5]

Not until the will of God was fulfilled, did Jesus finally submit his life as the atonement for sin and say, "It is finished." And we are told, "...He bowed his head, and gave up the ghost."[6]

Jesus, as in all things, is our faithful example. And so, surrendering ourselves to the will of God will allow for Joy and peace in the most difficult of rogue events.

Honey bees are one of God's wonderful marvels. They are such curious little creatures. One important service they render is the incredible labor of pollination. It would be a catastrophe to vegetation if this humble work was not performed. Farmers like to say of the honey bee that never has so much depended on so little. Let us consider the honey bee and what a marvel it truly is.

This little creature can organize a city (hive), build ten thousand cells for honey, twelve thousand cells for its larvae, and a holy of holies for the queen bee. This marvelous creature can create a system of ventilation to cool the hive, and travel twenty miles a day in search of nectar. That is impressive.

And the way bees tend to their young is fascinating. When the honey bee is in the first stage of growth, it is placed in a hexagonal cell with enough honey to insure maturity. Then the cell is sealed with wax. When the honey is exhausted by the newly formed bee, which is the signal to emerge from its cell. But coming out of the cell is not an easy chore. The young bee will have to struggle, wrestle, and strain, to get through the wall of wax.

Now, the question is this: Why is the exit not easier, rather than difficult? The exit is difficult because there is a purpose behind the struggle. The trial of its exit is necessary. You see, in the agony of pushing through, the infant honey bee rubs off the membrane that hides its wings. Once on the other side, it is able to fly.

Like the honey bee, we too, are born into a world that calls for the necessity of trials. If ever we stop pushing ahead, persevering through the agony of physical and spiritual trials, then all hope is gone. God expects us to push the limitations of our boundaries and reach beyond ourselves. Our wings, as it were, come as a result of surrendering to his will and way. Too many Christians attempt to persevere through trials with clipped-wings. They have never learned to trust Jesus in the difficult times, the rogue events of life. Strength to endure comes from the Lord when we surrender to his will. The Psalmist said:

> *"I will lift up mine eyes unto the hills from whence cometh my help. My help cometh from the Lord, which made heaven and earth. He will not suffer thy foot to be moved: he that keepeth thee will not slumber...The Lord is thy keeper...The Lord shall preserve thee from all evil: he shall preserve thy soul."[7] Psalms 121:1-8.*

The Bible tells us that, "...we must through much tribulation enter into the Kingdom of God."[8] How can we pass through a rogue event without a surrendered heart and life? We can look to Jesus who is our example, the One who surrendered to the cross.

Yes, He suffered and died for the sins of the world.

Yes, He was buried.

Yes, He rose from the dead.

But when angels rolled away that great stone, the pathway to heaven was made straight and true.

The seal of life and death was broken.

Our exit out of this world was guaranteed.

Flight into the heavenly realm was now possible.

But on this side, we must still learn the discipline of a surrendered will to the Lordship of Jesus Christ. And discipline comes to us through the trials of life as we surrender to his perfect will.

Why must I surrender to God's will in my life? We surrender because God is not satisfied with a halfway life. God desires a perfect work. When he is finished with you and me, God wants to see spiritual maturity and wholeness. In the hands of God the suffering of our trials develops endurance which results in spiritual maturity.

Now, this should not strike us odd that in our spirit-life we need the exercise of trials to strengthen our walk with the Lord. This same process works in the physical realm. If we need to build our cardiovascular stamina, we need to walk or run. To lose weight, we need to eat properly and learn to do "push-aways." To strengthen muscle tone, we need to lift a few barbells. Again, I'm reminded of the words, "no pain, no gain."

The reason many of us choose not to walk, or run, or lose weight, or tone those flabby muscles, is simply this: We just can't bring ourselves to surrender to the pain, or the agony, or the struggle, or the discipline, or even the time. *It's all a matter of the will.* All too often, we are sanctified and satisfied in our walk with the Lord. We see no need to inconvenience ourselves toward a deeper relationship with Jesus Christ. Hence, He sends the trials both small and great; to help us surrender to his will that strengthens our spiritual stamina.

Why do you need a surrendered will to the Lordship of Christ? Two reasons: First, God cannot build Christ-like character into your life without your cooperation; and second, God has a long-term goal for your life, it is called perfection.

Christ-Likeness

We are told: "But let patience have her *perfect work...*"[9] In other words, allow God to work through the trials of your life to accomplish His perfect work in your character. If you will cooperate with the Lord and recognize that He allows trials to temper your spirit, then in time you will experience the transformation of Christ likeness. Learn to surrender your life often to the Lord that He may accomplish his perfect will for your life. But if you resist, then God will chasten you into submission which will be more painful than a voluntary response. But the important thing here is this: God cannot work in us, the way He would like, without our consent. There must be cooperation; there must be surrender to His Lordship if we will develop Christ-likeness. Without our cooperation and submission, the danger is that our trials in life become meaningless. And we are forever muttering, "Why me, Lord?" In time, if you allow the trials of life to conform you into the image of Christ the proper question will be, "Why not me, Lord?"

In the Old Testament Jonah is a good example of someone who had trouble cooperating with God. He simply refused to surrender his will and subsequently, God chastised Jonah. We are told, "Now the Lord had prepared a great fish to swallow up Jonah. And Jonah was in the belly of the fish for three days and three nights."[10]

The question is, "Do you want the Lord to do his perfect work in your life? Letting Jesus dwell in you? Then you must refrain from resisting and refusing to cooperate with God's design for your life. God designed you to be like Jesus.[11] Why would you want to be anything less than the best God has for you? Paul the Apostle would say it like this, "...Christ in you, the hope of glory."[12] So, let us cooperate and surrender to Him, to His will, and experience the divine character of the blessed Christ upon our own hearts and lives.

Trials Materialize Life's Goal

You surrender to the will of God because through the trials of life we attain God's purpose and direction in life. Scriptures read: "...that ye may be perfect and entire, wanting nothing."[13]

Yes, the non-Christian can learn from the mishaps and pains of life, but how much better when we cooperate with him whose ultimate goal is to forge our hearts as one with his heart. God's goal for the believer is to mature in spirit. To grow and mature in faith; strengthening of the spirit is singularly important to God. Important because, "Without faith," we are told, "it is impossible to please God."[14]

How does one begin this quest, this process to develop God's goal in ones life? If the trials of life will materialize God's goal, then let us say these three things in regards to the above question:

> *First, there is the work God does for you: He saves you.*[15]
>
> *Second, there is the work God does in you: He sanctifies you.*[16]
>
> *Third, there is the work God does through you: He allows us the privilege to serve Him.*[17]

One of the wonderful things we learn about our Lord is that He is patient and longsuffering with our maturing process; He knows all too well how often we fail in our faithfulness to him.

Think about the longsuffering and patience of our God: He took twenty-five years in His work with Abraham before He allowed Abraham to have Isaac; He worked thirteen-years with Joseph before he allowed him to sit second to the throne of Egypt; God spent eighty years getting Moses ready for forty years of service; He took three years training his disciples; Paul the Apostle spent three years in the Arabian desert before God sent him out as the missionary to the Gentile nations. Yes, God is not in a hurry when it comes to your spiritual growth. The God who saved you is resolved to complete in you his goal and his plan for your life. One day, God desires to see you standing perfect in his sight.

The third key is a surrendered will to the Lordship of Jesus Christ which is developed through the process of becoming more like Christ through the permissive trials of life. When you learn that a surrendered will is necessary to endure our really bad days, our rogue days——then there will be meaning in your suffering. And your prayer will be: "Not my will be done, but thine be done."

The end

4

The Fourth Key:
A Heart That Wants to Believe

Apparently the Christians to whom James wrote had problems with their prayer life. James addressed this issue. He said:

> *"Ye ask, and receive not, because ye ask amiss, that ye may consume it upon your lust...Is there any among you afflicted? Let him pray. Is any merry? Let him sing psalms. Is any sick among you? Let him call for the elders of the church; and let them pray over him, anointing him with oil in the name of the lord: And the prayer of faith shall save the sick, and if he hath committed sins, they shall be forgiven him."*[1]

We should understand that "lack of prayer" is a sign of immaturity. Other basics of the faith include Bible study, church attendance, and commitment to good works. We must attend to the basics of our faith if we will know the joy of his Presence in our trials of life. And so it was that James drew the attention of these early Christians to the most fundamental aspect and practice in their walk with the Lord, the practice of prayer. Or, what we will call: A heart that wants to believe.

Back in the 80's, the medical community got very excited about the development of an artificial heart called, "The Jarvik 7." You might remember a man named Barney Clark who lived "112" days with this device implanted in his chest. Another man, William Schroeder, lived "620" days. Today the Jarvik 7 is used only as a temporary pump while a patient waits for a real heart.

Did you know that an estimated 100,000 Americans suffer from end-stage heart failure each year? And on the average only around 2000 hearts are available. But there is some good news for those who need help. Recently, the Food and Drug Administration has approved an experimental battery powered artificial heart. It weighs 2-pounds and is about the size of a grapefruit. It is rechargeable every 30 minutes. Patients are expected to have a normal lifestyle and even participate in light sports. The bad news is, it will initially sell for $75,000 to a $100,000. Ouch!

It is no surprise that our last strategy of trial management centers on a heart that will believe God in times of rogue events. We have been told for years that negative stress is bad on the heart. Stress is related to high blood pressure, irregular heart beats, palpitations, skin problems, dry mouth, constricted blood vessels. The Bible concurs that stress is not a good thing: "A merry heart makes a cheerful countenance but by sorrow of the heart the spirit is broken."[2]

People can fall into two groups in times of stress: The first group is known as the "Roaring Lions." When these people get stressed, they act aggressive. You've heard of going postal? The second group is called the "Frightened Rabbits." These tend to react in an emotional, tearful way and run from their troubles. But James offered a third group, those who pray. They respond to stress with a prayerful heart that wants to believe God and desires the promise of his peace:

> *"And the peace of God, which passeth all understanding, shall keep your hearts and minds through Christ Jesus."*[3]

Into which group do you fall? Roaring lions? Frightened rabbits? Or, the group that takes their troubles to the Lord in prayer? In a rogue day the supernatural peace of Almighty God is available through intercessory prayer.

If your walk with the Lord lacks prayer, you need to first ask Christ to forgive you and then begin immediately to practice these next three spiritual disciplines: Be Wise. Be Persistent. Always ask in faith.

Be Wise

First, a believing heart is developed as we are wise about the discipline of prayer. In times of distress and rogue events, we need a heart that grows stronger through meditation and communication with the Heavenly Father.

Not a week ago, I was scheduled for a certain procedure with the urologist. It was my first time to experience a prostate biopsy. Many men my age finds themselves going through this life saving technique. Weeks prior to this test, I walked alone and talked with the Lord. I asked for strength to endure it. I asked others to pray. When the day of the procedure arrived, I had prayer intercessors who sat with me. They wanted me to be spiritually prepared. And I was. In less than twenty minutes, I was done. And afterwards, there was relief, yes, but also joy that I was calm and reconciled to the will of God in this experience. It was something I had to endure. The point is, I was strengthened in my heart (my will) through prayer meditation and communion with the Heavenly Father.

Reading reliable material on the subject helps one to be wise. As it would happen, a dear Christian man found a book entitled, "How to Survive Prostate Cancer" by Patrick Walsh, a leading pioneer in prostate research. Can you believe it? He found the book in a public library for fifty cents. The Lord works in mysterious ways. Yes, He wanted me to pray, to lean on him, but The Lord also wanted me to be informed of the nature of this trial. This book and other material allowed me to be wise. In many ways, this knowledge helped to calm my trepidations that I might trust The Lord with the results. Prayer is a wonderful resource in the middle of rogue events. Remember, Prayer releases the power of God.

The Bible tells us: "If any of you lack wisdom (spiritual discernment), let him ask of God, which giveth to all men liberally..."[4] Our author makes it clear that praying is not optional, but optimal as we seek to triumph in our trials. We are to pray for wisdom in rogue events.

The Bible is adamant about this matter of prayer.

"Seek the Lord," we are admonished, "and his strength, seek his face continually."[5]

Our Lord was careful to stress the importance of prayer: "Ask, and it shall be given you; seek and ye shall find; knock, and it shall be opened unto you (Matthew 7:7)...Men ought always to pray. And not to faint."[6]

In his darkest hour in the Garden of Gethsemane, Jesus turned his heart to prayer. He told his disciples: "Sit here, while I go and pray..." And we are told, "And being in agony he prayed more earnestly: And his sweat was as it were great drops of blood falling to the ground."[7]

Paul identified prayer as an armament of spiritual warfare. He said: "Praying always with all prayer and supplication in the Spirit..."[8] You lack a tremendous resource if you ignore the ministry of prayer. Without prayer, you forfeit the strength that only God is able to give. You lack the ability "to be still and know that God is God." The Psalmist said: "Be still, and know that I am God: I will be exalted among the heathen, I will be exalted in the earth."[9] Rogue days rob us of peace, security, joy, and we need the peace of His Presence that comes through the discipline of prayer.

In the British Navy, whenever any sudden disaster happens, such as an explosion, it is the bugler's duty to play what is called, "The Still." When the men hear the bugler's call, they stop perfectly still and come to their senses before responding to the emergency.

The discipline of prayer is "Heaven's Still" for

the storms of life. It is hearing the commanding voice of the Master shout, "Peace Be Still." We are never wiser than when we take it to the Lord in prayer. When the trials of life explode and threaten your emotional and spiritual sanity, you are to stop what you are doing, get perfectly still, and seek the Lord in prayer. In prayer God shows us the way we should go, he gives the assurance of His sovereign control over our lives. The discipline of prayer is important. In the practice of prayer you attain the wisdom that you are not alone and the assurance that Emmanuel is with you.

Recently, I counseled with four couples. The common dilemma, or pattern of defeat, that plagued each relationship was infiltration of the pagan culture in which they lived, and of spiritual intimacy with God and each other. Ultimately, this two-punch knockout so battered and bruised the relationship that there was nothing to salvage. In each case, the woman left the husband. As the spiritual head of his family, these men had failed.

Make no mistake, without Jesus Christ strengthening the inner spirit of a man or woman, the paganism around us and the lack of Godliness in us will undo what otherwise could have been a beautiful life under the Lordship of Christ.

Perhaps you are going through a separation, a divorce, or you have fallen out of love. The only remedy to be offered is this: Be wise. Recognize your real enemy. Apply yourself to the basics of the Christian faith. And above all, clasp the hand of the one God gave to you and pray the power of God to sanctify your relationship: First with God and then to each other.

Be Persistent

Next, a believing heart is developed as we are wise about the persistence of prayer. Never stop asking God for what you need most, wisdom.

James said: "If any of you lack *wisdom*, let him ask God."[10] James is making reference to "spiritual insight." Believers must be persistent in seeking and requesting greater insight into the workings of God in their lives. We need this higher wisdom to discern how our trials merge into God's plans for our lives. Apparently, this wisdom is a spiritual gift because we are encouraged to pray and ask for it.

Why not ask for strength, or grace, or even deliverance in our trials? Why wisdom? It is okay to ask for these things, but we must have spiritual understanding from the Lord if we will endure our trials and not waste the opportunities of tempered faith. Without spiritual knowledge the number one question asked when the trials come is, "Why me, Lord?" And so we are told how to pray. Pray for wisdom.

We are admonished to pray with a believing heart asking in faith. "But let him ask in faith," James said, "nothing wavering..."[11] The enemy against answered prayer is unbelief. If we will pray, then let it be with the attitude that nothing is impossible with God.[12] Prayer is an act of faith in the ability of God to act on your behalf.[13] However, always keep in mind that God is not our heavenly bellhop, he answers prayer according to His perfect will, not our wills.[14] He may respond with a yes, no, or wait. And when you pray, pray to God your heavenly Father in the name of Jesus Christ. Christ is our great high priest who ever lives to make intercession on our behalf. Why would you pray and not invoke the authoritative name of Jesus Christ? In John 14:6, Jesus made it quite clear that "No one comes to the father but by me."

Now three things happen when you do not pray persistently; that is, praying in faith with a believing heart and seeking not your will, but the will of God in any given circumstance of life: Instability, lost of blessings, shallow commitment.

Instability

We read, "...For he that wavereth is like a wave of the sea driven with the wind and tossed."[15] A man that doesn't give himself to prayer will be unstable in all his ways, like a cork on a tempest sea. First the cork is blown in one direction, and when the wind changes course the cork is compelled to follow in another direction. It could suggest the picture of a drunkard who staggers from one side of the road to the next, lost and oblivious to direction. Such a person is going nowhere. But prayer is like an inner gyroscope, and helps a man to find stability even in the worst of days.

Loss of Blessings

Then, we are told that lack of prayer circumvents the blessings of God on your life: "For let not that man think that he shall receive anything of the Lord."[16] When you don not trust God, it is an insult cast in His face and you remove yourself from the place of blessing. You essentially become un-bless-able.

A Shallow Commitment

Lack of prayer means a lack of commitment to the Lord: "A double minded man is unstable in all his ways."[17] Literally, a life without prayer makes a shallow believer because you are given to vacillating between your desire to trust or doubt the Lord. In a sense, you become a walking civil war within yourself.

And so a spiritual heart, a heart that will believe and trust Jesus, is our last key to overcoming a rogue event. Such a heart is developed through prayer, persistence in prayer, and commitment to the Lordship of Jesus Christ over your life.

As we come to a conclusion on this subject of overcoming a rogue event, James gives to us the results of following these four management trials strategies. James wrote:

> *"Blessed is the man that endureth temptation: for when he is tried, he shall receive the crown of life, which the Lord hath promised to them that Love him."*[18]

As one applies the four management strategies of a joyful attitude, an understanding mind, a surrendered will, and a believing heart to a rogue event, certain rewards are to be expected:

> *Happiness, "Blessed is the man..."*
>
> *Endurance, "...endureth temptation..."*
>
> *Fuller life, "...crown of life..."*

A deeper love for the Lord Jesus, "...which the Lord hath promised to them who love him."

The end

5.

The Rogue Day Called Death

The rogue day called death is the one event, especially on an emotional level, that we find utterly difficult to manage. Who would find death a welcomed guest? And yet death comes, the great divider of hearth and home.

As a pastor I love my church family and care for each soul deeply. They are God's people and that makes them very special and defines my responsibility to them. One of those responsibilities I am frequently called upon to minister is "death and dying." The pastor who loves his church family will always find the death of a church member as his own flesh and blood. And the sorrow of the family is shared.

But in this rogue event of life, there is the living hope, the hope of translation and regeneration for the child of God.[1] There is great joy when the victory of our Lord's resurrection is appropriated by those who have been born twice. Well it has been said: "Born once die twice, born twice die once."[2]

What the Bible Says About Death

> *"And as it is appointed once unto men to die, but after this the judgment: So Christ was once offered to bear the sins of many; and unto them that look for him shall he appear the second time without sin unto salvation."*[3]

Death is a subject only appreciated by those who have finally crossed the half-century threshold of life. In our fifties, we come to the despairing conclusion that it is only a matter of time before our material bodies self-destruct to make room for new life. A pushing to one side, as it were, so others can begin their journey. The thing is, time was all we ever had, but we are only more conscious of it as we age. Then we say "where has all the time gone?" But the indisputable fact of life is this: Death is a universal and common malady.[4] As our friend, Dr. Stephen Cherniske, reminded us in his book "The Metabolic Plan": "Then…we turn fifty, and double wham, we're gripped by the sense that the rest (of our worldly tenure) will include progressive disability, degeneration, and decrepitude——in other words, pain and suffering."[5] Every human being is hardwired via our genes to initiate a shutdown sequence which is punctuated by disability, degeneration, and decrepitude. It is true, as Mr. Cherniske teaches, that with proper nutrition and exercise one may (I emphasize may) extend their life to 120. But still, every man has a scheduled appointment: "…it is appointed unto men once to die..." And I suppose if death has any redeeming virtue, it would be mercy. As someone has said, "It would be a curse to live forever in this body of death."[6]

His name was Danny Potter, a young man in his thirties who loved life, who always had a smile on his face. Danny had the gift of wit; he was the kind of person who could bring laughter to those around him without a moment's notice. But Danny had a serious diabetic condition, one that eventually took his leg and eventually his life. In God's mercy, his body was no longer suitable to house his indomitable spirit. God called Danny home.

How many of us would want to live 200 years? Can you imagine the agony of sustained life in this age-sensitive vessel? No, we must reconcile ourselves to what life is and act accordingly: "For what is your life? It is even a vapor that appeareth for a little time, and then vanishes away."[7]

Since death is an appointment, one every human being must keep, let us speak to the subject in three ways: Death is a certainty; judgment is a reality; deliverance is a necessity.

Death Is a Certainty

The question might be proposed why we should ponder the objective truth that death is a certainty of life; after all, every graveyard is a neon reminder that death is among us. Yet, there is much deception on this very prominent event.

People read books on near death experiences. Books like "Embraced by The Light," by Betty Eddie, or a more recent book, "90 Minutes in Heaven," by Don Piper. Others give an audience to popular mediums, spiritualists who can speak to the dead. Others try to learn about the afterlife by so-called "physic researchers," who say they can reach the dead through séances. Still others, believe that death is the end of their existence, when you die you simply cease to exist. Some believe in reincarnation. They believe when they die they are recycled as something or someone. The cult of Islam boasts more than a billion adherents. The men believe if you live a righteous life (works and keeping regulations) you will inherit paradise and a harem of seventy-two virgins. Think about that! The afterlife is presented as a joyous polygamist affair throughout eternity (by the way, what do Moslem women get?).

But according to the Bible we have one chance in life and after that the judgment. The only true authority that offers enlightenment and assurance is The Bible. According to Scripture this mortal body does indeed die releasing the spirit of man to be present with the Lord.[8] When you come to that last great event, only the truth of God's Word will be able to offer you hope. The Bible says of itself: "All scripture is given by inspiration of God and is profitable for doctrine..."[9] Only God's inspired Word can spotlight the truth about death and help you to overcome the deception of pagan superstitions.

The Bible teaches the concept that there are three components to human life: Spirit, soul, and body.[10] The body is the instrument of physical life. It serves as a vessel for containment and a vehicle through which we can function in the material world, communicate one with the other, and serve God. We must have a body to be human, but this aspect of man eventually succumbs to the curse of sin.[11] In time the body degenerates, dies, and dissolves. Nevertheless, we have a body for the duration of this life.

The spirit/soul aspect of man is invisible and continues to exist after the death of the body. When we speak of the spirit of man, we are addressing something that connects mankind to his Creator. The Bible reminds us that in the beginning, "the Lord God formed man from the dust of the earth, breathed into his nostrils the breath of life, and man became a living soul."[12] This breath of life, the wind of God, caused the man to have spirit (Spirit can be translated "wind" from the Greek word pneuma). And since the Bible teaches that we worship God in "Spirit and Truth," we can clearly see our connection with our Heavenly Father.[13] Our spirit is what allows us to seek and acknowledge the existence of God. No other animal life is capable of conceptualizing the idea of God; much less offer him worship and adoration. Spirit generates awareness that man is not alone, that God is. And so man is a spirit-creature. The soul (translated psyche, or the psychological aspect) is that part of man that is able to show intellect, emotion, and will. The soul gives man the ability to think about God (intellect), to love God (emotion), and to volitionally humble oneself to His sovereign authority (will). It is soul that gives you personality, and it is the place where character is developed, whether it is Christ-like, or of this present world. In other words, soul is the "real you" locked inside the body, locked away until the appointed hour to render an account to God how you lived his life in the body.[14]

Knowing the above truth as to our creature-ness, (our singular difference of body/soul/spirit) a being that can contemplate its own demise, we cannot help but acknowledge that death is an in-your-face reality of this life. Since death is real, the question that begs to be answered is "what is my life? What significance and purpose do I have for even being born? Is my life all about death?"

Death is certain to every baby born of a mother's womb. God's grace and mercy is the only reason that life was not aborted instantaneously after the fall of the first human being, Adam.

Death is certain. But time has been allotted for every person to prepare to meet their God. No one is able to say, "But I needed more time." The scripture says "time was appointed."

Death is certain. The scriptures say, "It is appointed unto men once to die..." It is not "if" one will die, but "when" one will die. The question is not, "Can I cheat death?" but "What can I expect when death comes?" Some risk eternity on a death bed confession, but death has no thirty-minute buzzer to warn of its approach. When death comes, it comes abruptly...some might even say rudely. No time to pack your bags, leave a note, or say a kind word to loved ones. No, time is up! It is time to depart. But still, many are deceived and believe in a second chance after death.

Jesus made it clear in his parable of the rich man who died and went to hell that there is no second chance after death. In hell the rich man cried for help, but was told:

> *"...between us and you there is a great gulf fixed: So that they which would pass from hence to you cannot; neither can they pass to us that would come from thence."*[15]

Death is a certainty. And we should not be deceived by fables conjured in the minds of men. The Bible is the only reliable source on the certainty of death and our earthly preparation for it. Medical science is extending our lives with new surgical procedures and new medicines. But despite these advances, no one has discovered a cure for death. Again, the scripture say, "...it is appointed unto men once to die..."

Judgment Is a Reality

The certainty of death leads us to the second consideration: After death, according to Hebrews 9:27, we can expect judgment on how we lived our lives in these borrowed bodies.[16] I say "borrowed" because you and I cannot create, we can only procreate. Therefore, the Creator is responsible for these bodies, they belong to him, and he is gracious to allow us the use of them. But the passage reminds us, "...but after this the judgment."

Once we are separated from the body, an instrument that connects us to a time/space/material continuum, then our next stop is the judgment of God. We will be called to render an account how we used these bodies. Did we glorify God with righteous character, appropriated only through Jesus Christ? Or, did we squander its intended purpose upon our sinful lusts, acting as if these bodies are ours to do as we please?

There are two judgments we should be concerned with after death: One is called the Judgment Seat of Christ. And the other is called The Great White Judgment Throne of God.

On the Judgment Seat of Christ, we are told:

> *"For we must all appear before the Judgment Seat of Christ that every one may receive the things done in the body, according what you have done, whether it be good or bad."*[17]

This judgment is not about salvation because the Bible tells us, "There is now no condemnation to them which are in Christ Jesus..."[18] This judgment is scheduled for believers, followers of Christ, to determine our rewards for service rendered on behalf of the Lord.[19] Believers do not appear before this judgment bar to be judged for sin. The believer's sins have already been atoned for by our Sin Bearer, the Lord Jesus on a hill called Calvary.[20] It was there on the cross that He became sin for us and extinguished the wrath of God's vengeance against the ungodly.[21] The Bible says of him:

> *"But now once in the end of the world hath He appeared to put away sin by the sacrifice of Himself..."*[22]

I have always looked upon the Judgment Seat of Christ as a border crossing into The City of God for believers. Before crossing into the heavenly city, I visualize The Lord Jesus himself stamping our passport in the spotless blood of His atoning sacrifice and saying, "Well done, good and faithful servant...enter thou into the joy of thy Lord."[23]

Then there is The Great White Judgment Throne of God in the judgment hall of eternity. Tragically, this judgment is reserved for those who spurned and rejected Jesus Christ as God's perfect and ultimate solution to mankind's sin-problem. The Bible says:

> *"And I (John) saw a great white throne, and Him that sat on it, from whose face the earth and the heaven fled away; and there was found no place for them. And I saw the dead, small and great, stand before God; and the books were opened, which is the book of life: and the dead were judged out of those things which were written in the books, according to their works. And the sea gave up the dead which were in it; death and hell delivered up the dead which were in them: and they were judged every man according to their works. And death and hell were cast into the lake of fire. This is the second death. And whosoever was not found written in the book of life was cast into the lake of fire."* [24]

No one in their right mind would want to be a willing participant at this summons. And yet, in this life, everyone is destined for one of two destinations after death: Eternal bliss in the tender embrace of a loving Savior;[25] or, eternal damnation where there is only the memory of a miss-spent life, "where their worm dieth not, nor the fire is quenched."[26] In light of such a horrible judgment, who would want to gamble that at the end of one's life there is no God?

Deliverance Is a Necessity

If death is a certainty, and judgment is a reality, then deliverance is an absolute necessity. The word "appear" is used three times in Hebrews 9:24-28. This is significant because the word "appear" answers the question, "why we can be saved?"

In v.24, we can be delivered from the judgment of sin because, "Jesus Christ has *appeared* into heaven itself *now* in the presence of God for us." He is our great High Priest who *now* ever lives to make intercession for those who have called upon his name for salvation.[27] The implication is, one of our own kind *now* resides before the very throne of Almighty God. That is, humanity has a human advocate who is continuously before the bar of God assuring that Judgment has been passed-over those who have made peace with God through the blood of the cross. The scriptures say:

> *"And if any man sin, we have an advocate with the Father, Jesus Christ the Righteous: And He is the propitiation for our sins: And not for ours only, but also for the sins of the whole world."*[28]

This is tremendously important. If one of our kind has not overcome death, hell, and the grave (which Jesus Christ did in his resurrection) then we have no advocate to plead our case before the Judge Of The Ages and all hope is gone. Death does indeed reign supreme and we are lost in all our guilty sins. And the human race has no future. We are doomed to extinction.

One of our Lord's favorite titles is "Son of Man," which suggest that Jesus Christ is our Kinsman Redeemer after the flesh. He is God with skin on his face. One of our own has made it to Heaven and that simply means: If one us is now appearing in the very Presence of our God, then the path has been blazed so that others of our kind may follow and also appear in that celestial city.

Deliverance is a necessity. And the hope that brings that deliverance is to be had in a Savior who now appears for us in the very Presence of God.

Further, in v.26, we can be delivered from the judgment of sin because "He has *appeared* to put away sin by the sacrifice of himself."

We are speaking here of the vicarious atonement of Jesus Christ; that is, His substitute death on the cross for the forgiveness of sin, "the just for the unjust."[29] Whether one wishes to debate or argue the necessity of the death of Christ, or the shedding of Christ's blood for eternal salvation, that is one's prerogative; however, like Peter, only one question is of utmost importance: "Lord, to whom shall we go? Thou has the words of eternal life."[30] We are free to question the person of Jesus Christ, His blood atonement, and the efficacy of so great a sacrifice. But in the end, when death makes its midnight call, what then? And to whom will *you go?*

The Good News is this: In faith we can believe that God has provided a way to satisfy his own unalterable just nature, a just integrity which demands that our sins be judged.[31] And God has made this way of acquittal possible in the death of Jesus Christ. Our Lord said himself: "If you believe not that I am he, you shall die in your sins."[32] What did our Lord mean, "if we believe not...we would die in our sins?" Categorically, He meant "Without the shedding of blood there is no forgiveness of sin."[33] Atonement means he took our place, our sins, and died our death, so we could be delivered from the same. And having secured your deliverance he reconciled you to God by his blood, the blood of the only sinless human being who ever lived among men.[34] He was Emmanuel, "God with us in human flesh."

Deliverance is a necessity. And the hope that brings that deliverance is to be had in a Savior who has appeared to put away sin by the sacrifice of himself.

Then in v.28, we can be delivered from sin because one day soon, "...unto them that look for him shall he appear the second time without sin unto salvation."

The return of Jesus Christ is the blessed hope of every believer. The scriptures say:

> *"Looking for that blessed hope and the glorious appearing of the great God and our Savior Jesus Christ; who gave himself for us, that He might redeem a peculiar people, zealous of good works."*[35]

The blessed hope of Christ's return is the hope of the ages. Only in this special act of God will the world be completely able to experience the overthrow of evil and establishment of righteousness, peace, and joy peculiar to the Kingdom of God on earth. To believe that man eventually will be better, and do better, is a delusional hope, a false hope. The world is destined for ruination. If the first eleven chapters of Genesis teach us anything, it is that without God mankind is doomed to failure. Mankind has a fatal malady. It is called "sin." And as long as sin reigns in his mortal body, it will not be paradise but pandemonium that best characterizes this world.

For believers, the return of Christ is a sanctifying hope. "Every man that hath this hope in him," we are told, "purifieth himself, even as he is pure."[36] Further, the question is asked, "...what manner of persons ought ye to be in all holy conversation (behavior, conduct) and godliness, looking for and hasting unto the coming of the day of God?"[37] When one reconciles themselves to the truth that "This same Jesus, which was taken up from us into heaven, shall so come in like manner..." such astounding truth has the power to change the way you live and conduct your behavior. The expectation of His "coming again" has a sanctifying power in the lives of believers.

For those who are unconcerned about the return of Christ to the earth, and there are many, I would say to you that this blessed hope is both *sure* and *significant*.

The blessed hope of His coming is a sure hope because both the Old Testament and New have predicted his coming. The Book of Job, possibly the oldest book in the Bible, said: "I know that my Redeemer liveth, and that He shall stand at the latter day upon the earth."[38] The old prophet Zechariah prophesied: "...and His feet shall stand in that day upon the Mount of Olives...And the Lord shall be King over all the earth."[39] The Psalmist declared that, "When the Lord shall build up Zion, He shall appear in His glory."[40] Daniel foresaw the establishment of this future Kingdom through an act of war when Messiah, like a great stone, would destroy the ungodly nations and rule the earth.[41] Isaiah tells us that this king coming will be a man, but not any man. He introduced this man as the Son of God when he wrote:

> *"For unto us a child is born, unto us a Son is given, and the government shall be upon his shoulders, and his name shall be called*

> *Wonderful, Counselor, the Mighty God, the Everlasting Father, the Prince of Peace. Of the increase of His government there shall be no end, upon the throne of David, and upon His Kingdom to order it, and to establish it with judgment and with justice from henceforth even evermore."*[42]

The New Testament is equally adamant about the sure return of Jesus Christ. Luke reminded the hearers of his day that, "The powers of heaven shall be shaken. And then shall they see the Son of Man coming in a cloud with power and great glory."[43] Jesus Christ said Himself, "I will return again."[44] So powerful and sure is this theme of the second coming that the last words of the Bible warn: "Surely I come quickly."[45]

History has always been tottering on the edge of ruin. The extinguished glories of past nations are buried in the bone yard of "no more." And except for the redemptive love and grace of Almighty God, the world as we know it would have ceased long ago. Today, once again, we are confronted with the demise of civilization, specifically western civilization. This time evil comes to us in the form of rabid Moslem extremism, or what we have labeled as terrorism. And indeed, these misguided souls (if they are anything), surely are a terror. There can be no worse evil than evil garbed in a religious cloak; the proverbial wolf in sheep's clothing.[46] Whatever mischief of evil this threat brings to the nations of the world, it will come to naught before the coming of the King of kings.[47] The coming of Jesus Christ is sure.

The blessed hope of his coming will be significant for both believers and unbelievers: For believers the coming of Christ will be triumphant. For unbelievers it will mean the most horrendous tragedy imaginable. Speaking of His coming Jesus said:

> *"As the days of Noah were, so shall also the coming of the Son of man be. For as in the days that were before the flood they were eating and drinking...and knew not until the flood came... so shall also the coming of the Son if Man be, Then shall two be in the field; the one shall be taken, and the other left. Two women shall be grinding at the mill; the one shall be taken, and the other left."*[48]

Before the great and terrible day of the Lord, believers will be rescued from the wrath of God coming upon the ungodly nations during the Great Tribulation period. Like the eight individuals who found safety in Noah's ark, likewise all those who trust Christ will be delivered from the wrath to come. This wonderful truth is shared by Paul in 1 Thessalonians:

> *"For the Lord himself shall descend from heaven with a shout, with the voice of the archangel, and with the trump of God: and the dead in Christ shall rise first: Then we which are alive and remain shall be caught up together with them in the clouds, to meet the Lord in the air: and so shall we ever be the Lord."*[49]

The coming of Christ is significant for born-again believers because it means only they will be spared the horrific judgment of the wrath of an angry God.

Not so with unbelievers. Those who ignored repentance of sin and denied Christ entrance into their lives will suffer what the Bible calls, "...the great winepress of the wrath of God."[50] In the Book of the Revelation, this awful time of judgment is described as follows:

> *"And out of His mouth goeth a sharp sword, that with it he should smite the nations: and he shall rule them with a rod of iron: and he treadeth the winepress of the fierceness of Almighty God. And he hath on His vesture and on his thigh a name written, King of kings and Lord of lords."*[51]

Those left behind are called the children of wrath. They chose to live their lives without God, without hope and faith in Jesus Christ. And tragically, they will be left behind to suffer the indignation of the wrath of God. But believers who "look for him shall he appear the second time" and deliver them from the wrath to come. That is why deliverance is a necessity. And so the coming of Jesus will be significant for both believers and unbelievers.

Death is certain, judgment is real, and our deliverance is a necessity. Accepting Jesus Christ as our Deliverer from sin by repentance and acknowledging him as the Son of God, we are forgiven and become the children of God. And when this rogue day of death finally comes, it is only an open door through which you will pass into a richer, fuller life where you are assured there is no more death. In Christ you can find peace in the expectation of death: The peace of passing from storm and tempest to an unbroken calm; the peace of waking up and finding yourself at the Father's House.

The end

6.

What Is Death Like?

Her name was Sue.

Her body had contracted leukemia.

Soon she would succumb to her appointed hour.

Sue was a wonderful Christian lady full of spunk and tenacity. She presented herself with an in-your-face honesty that was always refreshing. I continue to remember her with love and admiration.

The doctor said that the white blood cells in her blood indicated that she was no longer chronic, but had crossed the border into acute leukemia. As I sat by her bed, I'll never forget what she said to me. In a raspy voice, as she took my hand, she said: "My dear sweet preacher. I love you. And guess what? I'm gonna see Jesus before you." At times like this it hurts to speak, but I remember praying, "Dear Jesus, thank you for the hope of Heaven and the gift of eternal life." My dear friend was suffering. Shortly, she would be born into a new world, a new life, free from pain and earthly concerns. A life promised from the One who had no reservations calling himself "The Resurrection and the Life."

Like life itself this chapter is short. How can it be otherwise since the question itself begs more information than any mortal experientially can give? Knowledge fades into a fog of ignorance. Only faith in Jesus Christ offers light on a very dark subject. Only Christ has such knowledge what it is like to die and live again. He alone offers the singular hope against a day every human being must endure: The rogue day called death.

Jesus described the effect of his own death as a woman in labor, suffering pain until the moment of childbirth when travail is supplanted by the triumph of new life. He said:

> *"A woman when she is in travail hath sorrow, her hour is come: but as soon as she is delivered of the child, she remembereth no more the anguish, for joy that a man is born into the world."*[1]

Then The Lord said:

> *"And ye now therefore have sorrow: but I will see you again, and your heart will rejoice, and your joy no man taketh from you."*[2]

I will see you again. How wonderful. How comforting these words from the Savior's lips, *I will see you again.*

In Philip Yancy's book, "Where Is God When It Hurts," the author said that each of our individual deaths can be seen as a birth. "Imagine what it would be like," he said, "if you had full consciousness as a fetus and could now remember those sensations."[3] And then he continued to express the act of birth in relation to death:

> *"Your world is dark, safe, secure. You are bathed in warm liquid, cushioned from shock. You do nothing for yourself; you are fed automatically, and a murmuring heartbeat assures you that someone larger than you fills all your needs. Your life consists of simple waiting——you're not sure what to wait for, but any change seems far away and scary. You meet no sharp objects, no pain, no threatening adventures. A fine existence. One day you feel a tug. The walls are falling in on you. Those soft cushions are not pulsing and beating against you, crushing you downwards. Your body is bent double, your limbs twisted and wrenched. You're falling, upside down. For the first time in your life, you feel pain. You're In a sea of rolling matter. There is more pressure, almost too intense to bear. Your head is squeezed flat, and you are pushed harder, harder into a dark tunnel. Oh, the pain. Noise. More pressure. You hurt all over. You hear a groining sound and an awful, sudden fear rushes in on you. It is happening——your world is collapsing. You're sure it's the end. You see a piercing, blinding light. Cold, Rough hands pull at you. A painful slap. Waaaahhhh.*

Congratulations, you have just been born."[4]

If we are to explain death, let us understand it as we would understand birth: "On this end of the birth canal" as Yancey says, "death seems fearsome, portentous, and full of pain. Death is a scary tunnel and we are sucked toward it by a powerful force. None of us looks forward to it. We're afraid. It's full of pressure, pain, darkness...the unknown."[5] Then the author said:

> *"But beyond the darkness and the pain there's a whole new world outside. When we wake up after death in that bright new world, our tears and hurts will be mere memories. And though the new world is so much better than this one, we have no categories to really understand what it will be like. The best the Bible writers can tell us is that then, instead of the silence of God, we will have the presence of God and see Him face to face...Our birth into new creatures will be complete."*[6]

Let the rogue day of death come, for come it must.

It is our last enemy. But let the child of God know this: After the pain comes the greatest gain. And as you cross over the threshold of this world into the next, you will hear the One who sits upon the throne of His dominion say, "Well done thou good and faithful servant...enter thou into the *joy of thy Lord*... Behold, I make all things new."[7]

The end

7.

Heaven: The Journey Home

There was this real estate agent who was using the invigorating climate as a selling pitch to unload a piece of land. As he talked to the prospective buyer, he said, "You know, I was born in this neck of the woods and just yesterday was my two-hundredth birthday."

Later the buyer took the agent's assistant aside and asked, "Is he really that old?"

Calm, cool, and collected, the assistant took a deep breath of air and replied, "I couldn't say, I've only known him for some hundred-fifty years."

As a Baptist Pastor, I guess you could say I've been pitching for some years a choice piece of real estate. I've been plugging a wonderful place that the Lord Jesus called "My Father's House." So long ago he told his disciples:

> *"Let not your hearts be troubled: Ye believe in God, believe also in me. In My Father's House are many mansions: If it were not so, I would have told you. I go to prepare a place for you. And If I go and prepare a place for you, I will come again, and receive you unto myself; that where I am, there ye may be also."* [1]

Jesus taught his disciples that they were only passing through this transient life. Learn from it. Grow in grace and in knowledge of who I am. Enjoy the blessings from God. Do well. Be kind. Preach the Gospel. Evangelize. Grow the church. Be salt and light in an unbelieving world. But keep in mind this is not the best of all possible worlds.

Heaven is a real place, a choice piece of *real* estate as it were, made possible through Christ's death, burial, and resurrection. And when this life (in the body) is over there is a prepared place for those who loved and trusted Christ as their personal Lord and Savior. As we consider heaven, let's think of ourselves as on a journey. This journey is called Life. We are journeymen simply passing through the trials and tribulations of a wilderness land, making our way to the Father's House. Let us isolate some things needed as you anticipate and prepare for the journey home.

Abraham's Journey Home:
Do You Know Where You Are Going?

In our town there is a family restaurant that Cynthia and I frequent. Maybe you have one in your town. It is called The Cracker Barrel. On one side is the restaurant that has a big fire place against the wall. Cozy. And the other side has candy, toys, and curiosity items. One evening, I came across a small slate sign that caught my attention. It read: "Do You Know Where You Are Going?——God! This is possibly the most soul-searching question a person may ask themselves. When this life is over, "Do you know where you are going?" I think our options are limited: It's either "nowhere" or "somewhere." If it's *nowhere*, well then——let us eat, drink, and be merry for tomorrow we die. Extinction is our only reward. Life is a cruel fluke of protoplasm with no eternal significance or purpose for why we were even born. Yeah, let's throw one big party and go out with a "BANG!" Let's celebrate our fifteen minutes of fame and play "God." And then we are no more.[2]

But, what if——
What "if" there is more to life than meets the eye? The Bible does say, "Eye hath not seen, nor ear heard, neither has entered into the heart of man, the things which God hath prepared for them that love him."[3] What "if" we are just passing through this material world? And what "if" the intent for human life had always been to inherit a spiritual world? I think even simple logic entertains the reality that there must be a Heaven. Everything has a diametrical opposite? For instance, if there is cold, there is hot; if there is deep, there is shallow; if there is high, there is low; if there is truth, there is a falsehood; if there is sweet, there is bitter, etc. So why do we hesitate to logically deduce that there must be a spiritual realm if there is an earthly realm? A place called Heaven.

The answer is really quite simple: We simply choose to believe that earth-living is the best of all possible worlds. And many believe this despite the fact, "we all eventually self-destruct." Did you hear what I said? We live to die. What kind of life is this? Is our existence the cruel legacy of doom perpetuated from one generation to the next? A vaporous life where the only reward for the privilege of birth is the grave? I say to you, what makes us even get up in the morning?

But "what if" one of our own kind, a human being, had already crossed over into the spirit world? What would that mean for the rest of us? It means a four-letter word: "Hope."[4]

In the 15th century men argued about the possibility of there being a new world "out yonder" as they would say, "toward the west." After all, no one in their day had ever crossed so vast a body of water as the Atlantic Ocean. But despite the doubts, that somewhere there was a new and undiscovered world, one man trusted God and believed it was so. His name was Christopher Columbus.

On August 3, 1492, Columbus unfurled his sails and in faith pointed his ships toward the west. In his diary he wrote:

> *"I prayed to the Most High Lord about my heart's great desire and He gave me the spirit and the intelligence for the task...It was the Lord who put into my mind (I could feel His hand upon me) the fact it would be possible to sail from here to the Indies."*[5]

Columbus did accidentally bump into the New World and upon returning to Spain, he immediately gave his report to King Ferdinand and Queen Isabella:

> *"Your Majesty and your Highness! I have returned with glad news: There is land out yonder...I have been there and seen it with my own eyes."*[6]

There is a new world, yet to be discovered and inhabited by human beings. In The Bible this new world is called Heaven. And Jesus Christ is our heavenly Columbus who alone has journeyed and blazed a trail into that heavenly realm of which men can only dream. Jesus said to his disciples:

> *"Little children, yet a little while I am with you. You shall seek Me: And as I said unto the Jews, where I go, you cannot come or follow me now...And If I go and prepare a place for you, I am coming again, and receive you unto Myself; that where I am, there ye may be also."*[7]

Jesus Christ, the Son of God and Son of man, has made the ultimate and necessary journey into the place he called Heaven, the holy abode of God himself. And so there is a man, a human being, one of our own species presently in Heaven. He is the Son of Man in human form, but also Son of God divine in every way. And the scriptures say of him:

> *"...He ever liveth to make intercession for them. For such an high priest became us, who is holy, harmless, undefiled, separate from sinners, and made higher than the heaven... who is consecrated for evermore...For there is*

> *one God, and one mediator between God and men, the man Christ Jesus."*[8]

One of our own is in Heaven. And from that celestial shore, Jesus Christ sends the message:

> *"Let not your hearts be troubled: If you believe in God, believe also in me. In My Father's house are many mansions: if it were not so, I would have told you. I go to prepare a place for you. And if I go and prepare a place for you, I will come again, and receive you unto me; that where I am, there ye may be also."*

There is a glorious future that awaits all God's children. A future more glorious than all our dreams awaits us in the "City which has foundations, whose Builder and Maker is God."[9]

Many apparently have a low estimation of human life, but mankind is the crown genius of Almighty God. The Psalmist said that man was wonderfully and fearfully made.[10] By His own hands, He scooped up the primordial earth and molded man's material form. And by his unworldly breath, divine wind, God breathed life into this earthen vessel. And behold, the man became a living soul.[11] This makes Mankind a unique creation because he was created in the image of his Maker.[12]

I choose to believe I'm going somewhere. Unlike a prairie hen, made to scratch out a living in the dirt, man was made in the image of His God, like an eagle souring he was meant to inhabit the high places. I choose to believe that "somewhere" is a place called Heaven; a new world out yonder for those prepared to claim it by faith.

And so, the question is, "Do you know where you are going?" Where is life taking you? Will it be a dead end? Or will it be a destiny beyond your wildest imagination.

The Call to Be a Traveling Man

When I was a kid, I used to hear a song on the radio written by Randy Daugherty entitled, "I'm a Traveling Man." As I remember, it was Ricky Nelson with his velvet croon who did the song justice. I can still hear myself in the shower, "Hey! I'm a Traveling man. Yeah! I'm a traveling man." Outside the bath room door the family dog would join right-in with perfect two-part harmony. Well, anyway, it sounded good to me. And the dog.

Do you remember Abraham in The Old Testament? He was a traveling man. His was a God-called life "to get out of thy country, and from thy kindred, and from thy father's house, unto a land that I will show thee."[13] Abraham was to be the progenitor of the Hebrew people. God told him:

> *"And I will make of thee a great nation, and I will bless thee, and make thy name great; and thou shalt be a blessing."*[14]

To accomplish what God wanted to do, Abraham had to become a *traveling man*. The Book of Hebrews tells us, "...and he went out, not knowing where he was going."[15] But God gave Abraham a promise: One day when his earthly wandering was over, he would enter a city which hath foundations, whose Builder and Maker is God.[16] But during his traveling days, Abraham would build a Hebrew nation, develop a spiritual relationship with God, be tried and tested, claim Canaan land, and receive a covenant.[17]

You probably don't think about it, but aren't we all on a journey, like Abraham, traveling to the Father's House? The mass of desperate men do not look at life as a journey toward Heaven. The ungodly are blinded to an eternal destiny. For them, life is a dead end street with no God, no hope, and no eternal day. And yet, we are all earth-travelers going somewhere, trying to find our way.

Whether one accepts it, or not——we are looking for a Promised Land. Many are simply too worldly, too proud, too ignorant, or too ungodly, to admit that the Road of Life leads to a divine destiny. And so the Promised Land is the "here and now." But like Abraham, we're only camping on this terrestrial ball of dust called earth. And along the way, bless God, some travelers have learned; before it's too late, we're only passing through this wilderness world. Camp along the path to the Father's House, but never forget you were Heaven-born so you could be Heaven-bound.[18]

If you want to know where your travels will take you, if Heaven is in your future, understand you need a competent guide, someone trained who has already crossed over. I can only think of one man, Jesus Christ, who confidently said, "I am the way..."[19] Choose to ignore him at your own peril, it's your call.[20] But remember, he is the first of our kind to rise from the dead. Look through history, if you will, you'll find no other who could say with authority, "I am the Resurrection, and the Life: He that believeth in Me, though he were dead, yet shall he live."[21] The major religious figures throughout history have no record of saying they would rise from the dead. Indeed, if you can find their graves, you'll find their bones. Don't fool yourself, we all live in the land of the dying, looking for the land of the living. We each need a guide to lead the way. We're all going somewhere. Are you ready to cross over? Remember: "...it is appointed unto men once to die, but then the judgement."[22] Why wait until the last minute to embark on the road of life called "Narrow Way?"[23] For a journey of this significance and magnitude preparation is needed.

Are you a traveling man on his way to the Father's House? If you are, let's go together. And while we're at it, join with me, if you will, in one of my favorite songs: "Hey, I'm a traveling man. Yeah, I'm a traveling man."[24]

A Path Called Trust and Obey

Have you ever heard of "Wrong Way Corrigan?"

In 1988, Douglas Corrigan who was 81 flew to Dublin, Ireland, as an honored guest for three days of ceremonies commemorating a flight that he flew fifty years earlier. His flight in 1938 became a legend.

On July 17, 1938, Douglas Corrigan took off from New York's "Brooklyn's Floyd Bennett Airfield" in a tiny single-engine plane. Corrigan had filed a flight plan for Long Beach, California, but 29 hours later he arrived in Dublin, Ireland, claiming his compasses had failed and that he had accidentally flown the wrong way.

"My compass froze," Corrigan explained. "I Guess I flew the wrong way." From that day forward, "Wrong Way Corrigan" became a commonly used term to describe anyone going in the wrong direction who believed he was going in the right direction.

"Wrong Way Corrigans" abound in every generation who are content to travel life's path in the wrong direction.[25] Many are beguiled by the sirens of "eat, drink, and be merry." The Bible tells us that, "There is a way, which seems right to a man, but its end is the way of death."[26] There is the wrong way of abstinence and disobedience. If you will travel the Narrow Way, in God's direction, you've got to walk the path of obedience.

The Bible tells us that, "By faith Abraham... obeyed; and he went out..."[27] Abraham teaches us that the journey of life is a pathway paved with obedience to God's Word.

Trust and Obey
When You Don't Know
Where You Are Going

Abraham obeyed when he didn't know *where* he was going. We are told:

> *"By faith Abraham, when he was called to go out into a place which he should afterward receive for an inheritance, obeyed; and he went out, not knowing where he went."*[28]

When God called Abraham out of his country, He called him away from his family, friends, and the familiar. Abraham's response was one of obedience by faith. He simply took God at His Word and obeyed. The promise was given, "And I will make of thee a great nation, and I will bless thee, and make thy name great; and thou shalt be a blessing."[29] God honored His promise and blessed

Abraham's obedience: He became the father of the Hebrew nation.

As it comes to Heaven, like Abraham, our response must be one of trust and obey. We must trust Christ at his word that there is such a place and that He has gone ahead to make ready this abode of the saints. No living human (except the Lord Jesus, of course) has ever been to this extraordinary place of other-worldliness and unimaginable splendor. And this is one reason that we must trust and obey what he has said about this heavenly afterlife.

Most of us are like common yard ants that scurry in the dirt, oblivious to everything except building mounds and hatching more ants; we are earth-dwellers, concerned with home and hearth, with scarce thought of a place called Heaven. Earth is home and that's the end of it! If we can't see it, then it must not be. And so we are content to accept our lot and live out our days in stoic resolve and quiet despair scratching out a vaporous, short-lived existence, one filled with trials and tribulations of every sort.

No meaning for our lives.

No significance for our existence.

No hope of an Eternal Day.

But if we trust and obey in God's Son and his promise of Heaven, all that will change.[30] Suddenly, my life has destiny, meaning, significance, and most of all——*hope*. The hope of a new day dawning that earthen eyes have not seen, nor ears heard.[31] Because Heaven is real, my spatial life on earth is but a journey; an adventure toward the spiritual sphere of my Creator and Heavenly Father; a special place that Jesus Christ promised so long ago for the one who has ears to hear and an obedient heart. Did he not say: "And if I go and prepare a place for you, I will come again, and receive you unto myself; that where I am, there ye may be also?" Indeed He did.

Remember that you are a spiritual creature who dreams and yearns for a spiritual home, a home called Heaven. And if you will obey God's Word concerning the means of acquiring Heaven,[32] then you can be assured that God will be faithful to bid you entrance at the appropriate hour. Only trust and obey, even when you don't know where you are going. It's enough that the Lord Jesus knows. Don't be a "Wrong Way Corrigan." The path of life is not a dead end road. Set your compass by the Word of God and Trust Christ to be your Guide. Believe there is a place called Heaven. A place Prepared for you.

Trust and Obey
When You Don't know How
God's Will Can Be Done

Next, Abraham obeyed when he didn't know *how* God's will would be accomplished. We are told:

> "Through Faith also Sara herself received strength to conceive seed, and was delivered of a child when she was passed age, because she judged him faithful who had promised. Therefore sprang there even one, and him as good as dead, so many as the stars of the sky in multitude, and as the sand which is by the sea shore innumerable."[33]

When God called Abraham to serve him, He made a promise to Abraham: "I will make of thee a great nation..."[34] Abraham was to become the Father of the Hebrew people. All that was needed was the birth of a son. But as the years rocked along, no child was born. How was God's will to be accomplished without a son? Abraham was now one hundred years old and Sarah was ninety. Surprise! Sarah gave birth to a miracle baby. His name was Isaac, which means "laughter." And so, God kept his promise. His will would be accomplished. It wasn't necessary for Abraham to "know how," God would fulfill his will. The application of faith was the only response incumbent on Abraham. God had the plan, Abraham simply needed to trust and obey.

If there is anything to be known about the way God operates, it is that he works by a plan.[35] God is omniscience and has the ability of foreknowledge; which means, He has no difficulty in scanning future events and coming up with the right game plan.

God's plan is that sinners be saved and heaven-bound. You don't need to necessarily concern yourself with how God will accomplish this, or what Heaven is, you simply need to act in faith according to God's Word. If God says, "...confess with thy mouth the Lord Jesus Christ, and shall believe in thine heart that God hath raised him from the dead, thou shall be saved," then through "faith" you accept this as God's plan of salvation.[36] If Jesus Christ said, "...I go to prepare a place for you...that where I am, you may be also," then through "faith" you can claim that destination as your own.[37] The reason so many ignore faith in God and the rewards that come with the execution of such faith, is because they enjoy playing god themselves. It is faith in me, not faith in God.

Like Abraham, most people of faith suffer from a lack of godly patience. We tend to forget that patience is one of the nine fruits of the Spirit believers are to incorporate into their walk with The Lord.[38] We must learn to wait on the Lord.[39] But Fourteen years earlier, Sarah became impatient with God and so she ordered Abraham to sleep with Hagar, her handmaid. Apparently, Abraham had no problem obeying. And so, Hagar conceived a son. His name was Ishmael.[40] This decision to help God fulfill his promise revealed a total lack of faith and trust in God's ability. The whole conspiracy to usurp God's plan turned out badly; it always does when we decide to play god. And the results can be catastrophic.

This failure of faith gave birth to the Palestinian and Jewish conflict in our world today. Ishmael became the progenitor of the Arab race and it is he of whom the scriptures speak, "And he will be a wild man; his hand will be against every man, and every man's hand against him..."[41] Isaac, the chosen seed, became the progenitor of the Hebrew race from whence The Savior would be born. And so the two shall never meet, nor know peace. The Palestinian/Jew conflict is the world's most dangerous family feud. It is a sign of the nearness of the hour and heralds the soon return of Christ to the earth. So you can see that failure to trust and obey God always has drastic repercussions; if not immediately, then in the long term.

Just because you do not see a way out of your own calamity, and you are at a loss to see how God's will could be accomplished, that does not mean God is helpless. That you are hopeless. Remember, like Abraham and Sarah, in your most desperate moments of life, God has a plan. And "laughter" is waiting to be born. And Heaven is real. You don't have to know everything about it, to get there. But you will need faith, faith to take God at His Word and believe that Christ is the "one and only" who can validate your ticket into the habitat of The Heavenly Father.

Trust and Obey
When you don't know
When God will fulfill His Promises

Abraham believed God and yet, he died not knowing when God would fulfill his promises. We are told:

> *"These all died in faith, not having received the promises, but having seen them afar off, and were persuaded of them, and embraced them, and confessed that they were strangers and pilgrim on the earth. For they that say such things declare plainly that they seek a country. And truly, if they had been mindful of that country from whence they came out, they might have had opportunity to have returned. But now they desire a better country, that is, a heavenly: Wherefore God is not ashamed to be called their God: For He hath prepared for them a city."*[42]

To believe God means to trust him to keep his promises. Abraham, as well as the patriarchs, was promised a better country with countless descendants, and that "in thee shall all families of the earth be blessed."[43] These were the promises they saw and greeted them from afar.[44] God would fulfill these promises in His own good time and pleasure.

Abraham and the rest of the heroes of faith had no idea when God would fulfill his promises. But "not knowing when" did not diminish the trustworthiness of God. He took God at His Word and claimed for himself that the best was yet to come. Abraham did not need to concern himself with "when" the Lord would fulfill his promises, he simply needed the faith to trust and obey.

The call to faith means trusting God to keep his promises. Such as we are, creatures of the moment bound to a vaporous life, we must depend on the providential care and graces of God. So, if God promised Heaven, then one needs only to trust and believe. Such a hope takes the sting out of death and victory from the grave. Pain and suffering become bearable. But remember, above all things, that this great hope has a name, Jesus Christ, of whom it is written: "Which hope we have as an anchor of the soul, both sure and steadfast..."[45] Without him Heaven is like a mirage seen through a thousand-mile stare. Heaven is incomprehensible and unattainable. Trusting God means to trust in Christ's atoning work on the cross for one's salvation. You must be redeemed by the blood of Christ to enter heaven.

Heaven will come soon enough, it's not "if" only "when." You need only the faith to trust God to keep his promises. Do you trust in his promise of heaven?

In Don Piper's popular book, "90 Minutes In Heaven," he wrote of his experience of dying in a horrible car crash and being swept away into Heaven:

> "When I died, I didn't flow through a long, dark tunnel. I had no sense of fading away or of coming back. I never felt my body being transported into the light. I heard no voices calling to me or anything else. Simultaneous with my last recollection of seeing the bridge and the rain, a light enveloped me, with a brilliance beyond earthly comprehension or description. Only that in my next moment of awareness, I was standing in heaven."[46]

Don Piper's after death experience shows us the indisputable value of one man's faith to trust in the promises of God. Yes, the experience of heaven is highly subjective, but who of us would deny Mr. Piper his right to express his out-of-body phenomena? Faith in the promise of heaven, wherein is the city of God, gives us hope that the cessation of this physical life is not the end of things, only the beginning.

Steve Whitworth, a friend of mine, told the story of a young Christian lady, 46 years old, who was dying with cancer. Her name was Rhonda Naylor. Early that morning, the doctors applied their trade. Hope springs eternal. Perhaps there was a chance to free her from this dreaded disease. But surgery soon revealed that the cursed malignancy had spread like a vengeful plaque throughout her fragile body. All hope to spare Rhonda's life had evaporated. Steve couldn't help himself as he wept over the desperate state of his dear friend. His heart ached as if squeezed by the unseen hand of hopelessness. Overwhelmed with grief, Steve reached out to Rhonda, he would comfort her, dredge up some random word of encouragement; perhaps God would grant him a stroke of inspiration that would speak to the moment. But it was then that God spoke through Rhonda: "Steve," Rhonda softly spoke, "Don't feel sad for me. I've been preparing my whole life for this."

Like Abraham, Rhonda didn't know when God would fulfill his promise of "where I am, thou shall be also," but as she said: "I've been preparing my whole life for this." The preparation of Rhonda's faith in Jesus Christ as her Savior made death an open door to the Father's House. We need to leave "when God will fulfill his promises," to God. Our concern must be to develop trust and obedience in god's Word because his promises are true. We need only learn to trust and obey.

One of the favorite characters in the Bible is a man named Joseph. His journey in life is a wonderful example of faith in God. As the Book of Genesis comes to a close, we learn from Joseph that delay is not God's denial.

Joseph is one 110-years-old and the time has come for him to die. He calls the elders of the children of Israel to come around him and makes them swear an oath that they will bring his bones out of Egypt into the Promised Land:

> *"And Joseph said unto his brethren, I die: And God will surely visit you, and ye shall Carry up my bones from hence. So Joseph died, being an hundred and ten years old: And they embalmed him, and he was put in a coffin in Egypt."[47]*

A hundred years passed and there was no keeping of God's promise. Yet Joseph had said, "God will surely visit you." Two hundred years passed, and three hundred years.

Three hundred ninety-five years passed. Still, there was no evidence of God's visitation. But at the end of four hundred years, according to the Word of God to Abraham, God appeared to Moses on the backside of the desert in a bush that burned unconsumed, and He sent Moses down to deliver his people.

Joseph trusted and obeyed. He didn't know when God would fulfill his promise, but fulfill it he did according to His own good time. And though the promise was long and delayed, it finally came to pass.

Can you trust in the promise of God about a place called heaven? Indeed you can. Only trust Christ to set you free from the condemnation of sin.

Trust and Obey
When You Don't Understand
How God Works

Abraham obeyed when he didn't understand how God was working or why He did what He did. Further, in Hebrews 11, we are told:

> *"By faith Abraham, when he was tried, offered up Isaac: And he that had received the promises offered up his only begotten son. Of whom it was said, that in Isaac shall thy seed be called. Accounting that God was able to raise him up, even from the dead; from whence also he received him in a figure."*[48]

The testing of Abraham's faith continued when he was commanded by God to sacrifice his only son, Isaac. The account of this trial is found in Genesis 22:17-19, where we see the superlative hallmark of Abraham's faith, or any man's faith. Abraham did not understand what God was doing. He couldn't comprehend why the Lord was directing him to slay his beloved son, the promised seed of his old age. How did Abraham trust and obey when the commandment of God seemed to clash with the promise of God?

Here is one of the elementary complaints shallow believers and unbelievers uses as an excuse to expunge themselves from their responsibility of acknowledging God. They say, "If there is a God, why does He allow horrible things to happen to good people?" Or, "How could a loving God allow me to suffer this awful disease? Or let this financial crisis ruin my life? How about the destruction of our marriage, my wife ran off with another man? How can I trust a God whom I am told loves me and at the same time allows me to suffer?"

And the list continues.

Of course, this perception that God should be our heavenly bellhop is absurd. God does love you. He loves the whole world.[49] but it is a mistake to think of Him as a doting grandfather. God's love is much deeper and far wiser. The truth is, as sons and daughters of God, God uses suffering to teach us obedience.[50] It is not that God brings suffering into our lives, but that He allows it. There is purpose in our afflictions——we need not necessarily discover that purpose——but like Abraham it is necessary as believers to remain steadfast in faith.

"Why," you ask? "Why should I stay faithful in the crises of life?" With a heart full of love, we maintain our faith in God because we lack the perfect understanding to know *how God works* and *why He does what He does*. Abraham chose to believe; yet, he harbored not a clue what God was doing, or why He was doing it. And yet, Abraham stayed on center trusting and obeying God.

Can you imagine how violated Abraham must have felt in his faith, and in his conscience? And how he felt in every natural paternal feeling? The moment Abraham raised the knife heavenward, ready to plunge it onto the chest of his beloved son, everything that was precious in life was about to die. Abraham could find no rhyme or reason to God's demand, it absolutely made no sense. This was the ultimate crisis that threatened to bulldoze a life structured on the foundation of faith in God. Another man, another time, the outcome may have been different, but "By faith Abraham..." chose to trust and obey. Simply astounding! In faith he walked through the valley of the shadow of death, and Abraham discovered life.

We can be assured that such a faith as Abraham's is rare and singular, indeed. But not to worry, God will never test your faith as He tested Abraham's faith; that is, the sacrificing of a son. But know that God will test you. Life, such as it is, contaminated by sin, is one filled with trials and tribulations. And God will use these conflicts and crises to challenge your faith in Him, because "Without faith it is impossible to please God."[51] Faith is the key to knowing God. More precisely, the key is your faith in Jesus Christ.[52]

Where are you right now? What crisis of life are you experiencing? The path called obedience may not be the easy way, but it will lead you in the right direction.

Do you know where you are going?

Jesus' Journey Home:
Do You Know Where He has Gone?

Every human being has two major goals to accomplish in relationship to God: First, there is our earthly goal to know God in the most personal and intimate sense. And second, there is our eternal goal to enter the divine domain of God called heaven. The latter is achieved by acknowledging Christ as our Redeemer, committing our heart and lives to the authority of His Word. Knowing God through the person of the Lord Jesus is the pre-requisite to the second goal, getting into heaven. Receiving Christ and becoming more like Him makes one holy, and the Bible reminds us that "without holiness no one will see The Lord."[53] Since heaven is a holy place, we must be holy if there is any hope of access into the habitat of God.

The subject, which we are presently interested, is our heavenly goal of entering the City of God, or heaven. When our life is completed, The Bible teaches there is a rest for the people of God. And that rest is not of this world. As we think about our eternal habitation, it is necessary to understand that one of our own has made heaven possible. If this is not so, then we are surely an enigma wrapped up in a puzzle.

On many occasions Jesus made reference to our being with him in heaven. He promised us: "That where I am, there you will be also."[54] Or, "...and where I am, there shall also my servant be."[55] And, "...be with me where I am that they may behold My glory."[56] It is clear from these passages and others that Jesus is looking forward to our arrival in heaven to be with Him forever. Jesus Christ is in heaven, but understanding what Jesus had to do to enter heaven is important to believers.

Embracing: He Chose the Nails

Bound up in our ability to choose is a bittersweet liberty. A decision initiated can be so sublime, so noble, and we hope so. Yet, how can we, finite as we are, know the ramifications and conclusions of the matter?

At 7:00 A.M. on July 11, 1804, Alexander Hamilton and Aaron Burr stood face to face, ready to settle their furious quarrel. They separated themselves by walking ten paces for the duel. Hamilton had already made the choice to fire into the air, a choice that would seal his fate. But the choice was his alone to make, a noble gesture, an olive branch Hamilton hoped Burr would haply receive. But the corrupt, scoundrel Burr shot Hamilton, the ball tearing through his liver, cracking a rib, and shattering a part of his spine. Thirty one hours later, one of the most brilliant political minds of the Republic was silenced. His was a wasted life with so much more to give to the Union he so cherished. The last words of Hamilton expressed his greatest concern: "If they break this union, they will break my heart."[57] But noble as it seemed, Hamilton made his decision, a choice that robbed history, too soon, of a great patriot. It was bittersweet, indeed.

Think, now, about bittersweet. He chose the nails. The Lord Jesus chose the way of sacrifice. His life given was propitiation for sin, a ransom of ONE for the many.[58] Embracing the cross, though designed from eternity, was a choice demonstrated in history. As one of us, a human being, the Lord Jesus could have said, "No, they're not worth it," and aborted God's redemptive plan for mankind. But the truth is, and The Lord Jesus said it himself, "...To end was I born, and for this cause came I into the world..."[59] The One born as The Sovereign over nations of men was the one born with a cross in his heart. Christ chose for his diadem a crown of thorns, a reed for his scepter, and a roman cloak for his robes of glory. But embracing the cross was a choice The Lord Jesus made. He made it not for himself, but for you and for me. He embraced the cross and chose the nails.

Bittersweet, indeed!

As the Son of Man the cross was bitter, he suffered beyond our scope of understanding. But as The Son of God, The Lord Jesus was in complete control. In three days he would rise from the dead, becoming the first of our kind to dwarf death's domain over the souls of men. The cross was the way home, back to heaven, back to heaven's throne that The Lord Jesus had abdicated 33 years before. And now, by virtue of his death, burial, and resurrection from the dead, the cross is our way to the Father's House. His choice had ultimate purpose for the human race. His embracing of the cross meant our liberation. His choosing of the nails was our salvation. The journey back home demanded a wounded Savior.

The flogging.
The beating.
The humiliation of slapping, spitting, laughter.
The nails, a spear, a crown of thorns.

This was the path of suffering predestined for Jesus Christ. His was a dark and lonely path through the valley of the shadow of death if heaven's door was to swing wide open for all men.

Such as we are by nature, children of wrath, heaven's door is locked and bolted, angelic sentries guard the way, and there is found no place for you and me in God's heavenly city. We are sinners. Death has conquered every man since the first seed of Adam. So, how could any man hope to walk through the valley of the shadow of death successfully and to be our own little savior?

You say, "I'm not such a bad person." We sympathize with such candor. But the problem is not that we can't do good things, we do. It's just that we can't keep from doing bad things. And that's why we need a hero, a shadow walker, who brings the light of life into the darkness of the valley of the shadow of death. Only Jesus Christ, the Son of Man, is blameless and sinless. Only he could embrace the cross, choose the nails, suffer the grave, but three days later rise bodily to conquer death and show others the way to heaven.

Submitting: He Obeyed
The Father's Will

The journey home for the blessed Christ meant being obedient to the bitter end. The Bible tells us that, "though he were a Son, yet learned he obedience by the things which he suffered. And being made perfect he became the Author of eternal life unto all them who obey him."[60] The road to the cross was a road of horrific sorrows and unimaginable suffering. But because the Lord Jesus embraced the cross and the agony of it, God the Father was glorified, His wrath satisfied, sins forgiven, and sinners were made sons and daughters of God. His perfect obedience to His Father's will, to His command, is the reason we can look forward to heaven.

In the North Pacific there is the island of Imo Jima. Its dry surface of volcanic ash has been likened to the landscape on the moon. For this tiny, but vital piece of land, we paid the price of some 21,000 casualties in our war with Japan. For the men who took it, it was never a question of adequacy or inadequacy, courage or lack of courage. They took the island in obedience to a command.

His journey home called for his unwavering obedience to become sin for the whole world. And He obeyed to the bitter end. In submission to His Father's will, Jesus allowed himself to become our substitute, the perfect Scapegoat, so we could by his merits enter the sanctity of the Holy City. Christ obeyed the Father's will.

Expressing: He revealed
God's Forgiving Love

The most wonderful passage in all The Bible is John 3:16:

> *"For God so loved the world, that He gave His only begotten Son, that whosoever believeth in him should not perish, but have everlasting life."*

This passage is wonderful because in Jesus Christ, God was glorified in Redeeming love. One cannot gaze upon the cross without seeing the "forever love," and the "forgiving love," of God reaching out to a lost world through the outstretched arms of Jesus Christ. Choose to look away, but in the God-man, Jesus Christ, God the Father has forever expressed his forgiving love toward mankind. His is a love that calls us to himself; that where he is, we may be also. He loved you so much that He chose the way of the cross to make a place for you in Heaven. He died loving you with his arms wide-open, when no one else could lift a finger. Someone's pen said it this way: "He drew a circle that shut me out: Heretic, Rebel, a thing to flout; But love and I had a mind to win; He drew a circle and took me in."

God has expressed the breath, the length, the depth, and the height of His redeeming love to every human being. We are without excuse. From the seven sayings of Christ from his cross, "Father, forgive them for they know not what they do," is the one that expresses so great a love, we can scarcely fathom the depth of it. Had the Lord Jesus not prayed this effectual prayer of love and forgiveness to His heavenly Father, the flood gate of God's tender mercies would yet be damned and barred.

But God honored the prayer of His Beloved. From the cross Christ expressed the magnanimity of His redeeming love to every human being so that we are without excuse.

Reclaiming:
His Pre-Incarnate Glory

In John 17, often called the "High Priestly Prayer," our Lord petitioned His Father for the glory he had before the world was. He said:

> *"I have glorified thee on the earth: I have finished the work which thou gaveth me to do. And now, O Lord, glorify thou me with thine own self with the glory which I had with thee before the world was."*[61]

Going home, back to heaven by way of His miraculous ascension, meant departing the limitations of personhood, place, time, and reclaiming the mutual and unlimited glory Jesus had known previously. It was time to reclaim his pre incarnate existence that belonged to him. And by saying "I have glorified Thee on the earth...," The Son of God was signifying he had accomplished the Father's will and glorified him by giving eternal life to those who would believe on him. His work was accomplished. It was time to go home.

What a wondrous excitement must have filled the spirit of our Lord. From eternity past Jesus joyfully existed in perfect God-glory, a glory of such cosmic scope and dimension we could never comprehend. God the Son voluntarily laid aside his royal diadem and eternal robe of glory for a crown made of thorns and a robe of flesh and blood. And he gave himself a special name, the name of Jesus.[62] And for the next thirty-three years, this spinning ball of dust that He created would be his dwelling place. But now it was time for heaven's Prince of Peace to petition the Father, and receive his preexistent glory that He had before the world was.

Jesus was in our world, a world he created, but he was not of this world. He had told those who could hear the truth that, "I am from above...I am not of this world."⁶³ He told Pilate on the eve of His crucifixion, my kingdom is not of this world..."⁶⁴ No one was listening. The perpetrators of the cross, no doubt, thought his death would be the end of him. Little could they have known that the way of the cross led Jesus home.

Can you imagine what it must have been like when Jesus finally arrived in heaven?

The first chapter in the Book of Acts recorded the ascension of our Lord. After speaking a final word to the disciples, that they are his witnesses, the law of physics was suspended and gravity released the Son of God. The disciples, awestruck, stretched their eye balls as the Lord was taken up bodily from the earth and a cloud received him out of their sight.

The planets and the stars humbled themselves and became his stepping stones as heaven's Darling made his way to the Father's house. Imagine the pearl gates swinging wide-open to receive the Lord Jesus. And outside those mammoth, pearl gates there are two antiphonal choirs of angels too numerous to count. On each side of the transparent street of Gold their voices are lifted high and thunderous. The first angelic choir shakes the foundations of the vast cosmos shouting: "Who shall ascend into the Hill of the Lord? Who shall stand in his holy place?"

The second choirs of angelic hosts shout back with an equally thunderous voice: "He that hath clean hands, and a pure heart; who hath not lifted up his soul unto vanity, nor sworn deceitfully."

Then the first antiphonal choirs, in a rapture response, trumpet their voices: "Lift up your heads, O ye gates; and be ye lift up, ye everlasting doors; and the King of Glory shall come in."

The second choir not to be outdone, begins stamping their feet, fluttering their great wings, and with a blast of orchestrated voices cry out: "Who is this King of Glory?"

To which the first choir, unable to contain themselves break forth with the glad tidings that all heaven has been waiting to hear: "He is the Lord strong and Mighty, the Lord mighty in battle...lift up the everlasting doors and the Lord of Hosts and King of Glory shall come in."[65]

Our ascended Lord continues on the gold, paved highway that passes through the celestial City of God. Abraham, Jacob, and Moses are there, among others, to welcome the Lord back home. "How are you, Lord? It sure is good to see you."

There are smiling faces on every side admiring the Lamb of God who died for the sins of the world. "Welcome home, Lord. You sure have been missed." The joy of seeing Jesus causes heaven's citizens to dance in the streets. Ecstatic jubilation fills the Holy City as worship and praise herald the coming of the King.

As the Lord Jesus made His way before the throne of God the Father, things begin to quiet down. Finally there is nothing but a holy hush of silence.

No angelic voices resonating in rapture praise.

No wings fluttering.

No dancing.

No applaud.

No further jubilation, only a stillness that baffles the senses.

The Lord Jesus has arrived before the throne of his Father for the purpose of claiming the glory which he had with the Father before the world was. From the Eternal Throne of Almighty God a voice reverberates as the sound of many waters: "What are these wounds in thine hands and by what right do you have to enter My realm of Glory?"

Then with outstretched hands, the Lord Jesus presents his wounds and says: "These wounds are those whereby I was wounded in the house of my friends."[66]

It is then that God the Father stands up from his throne. Every knee is bowed and every eye is closed as God the Father examines the tangible evidence of His Son's wounded form. Satisfied, the omnipotent voice of God, like a thousand crashing waterfalls, announces to a redeemed universe: "This is my son in whom I am well pleased. Come forward my beloved and inherit the glory you had with me before the world was."

At that very moment all heaven breaks out with heavenly applause and praise as the Lord Jesus takes his place at the right-hand of majesty and power. His work is done. And He is home, home at last.

Imagination is a wonderful tool for seeing where eyes cannot. But the truth here is this. Listen closely to what Jesus said: "And the glory which thou givest me I have given them; that they be one, even as we are one."[67] The glad news is this: Where Jesus presently is we have been promised that we will share in His glory.

The journey home called upon Christ to embrace the cross, submit to God's will, express God's love, and reclaim his glory. And His Home, because of His obedience, has become our home! Did He not say, "That where I am, there will you be also?"

Do you know where he has gone?

The Believer's Journey Home
Bound For the Promised Land

"On Jordon's stormy banks I stand,
and cast a wishful eye,
to Canaan's fair and happy land,
where my possessions lie.
There gen'rous fruits that never fail,
on trees immortal grow.
There rocks and hills and brooks and vales
with milk and honey flow.

All o'er those wide-extended plains
shines one eternal day;
there God the Son forever reigns
and scatters night away.

No chilling wind nor pois'nous breath
can reach that healthful shore;
sickness and sorrow and pain and death
are felt and feared no more.

When shall I reach that happy place
and be forever blest?
when shall I see my Father's face
and in His bosom rest?

I'm bound for the promised land.

I'm bound for the promised land.
Oh, who will come and go with me?
I'm bound for the promised land."[68]

This well known hymn written by the Rev. Samuel Stennett, 1787, son of a Baptist pastor, and pastor himself, has been a favorite of the faithful since its inception. The message it conveys is certainly one that every believer holds dear. This world is likened to Jordan's stormy banks, a world filled with the unrest of a sinful and sensate world. But just over the way is the unbroken calm of the Promised Land. It was this place that our Lord was to return, this place called heaven, after he finished his atoning work on the Golgotha's hill.

The shadow of the cross was now falling across the heart of the Lord Jesus. His time with the disciples was coming to a close and so he gathered them and announced, "Little children, yet a little while I am with you. Ye shall seek me: And as I said unto the Jews, whither I go, ye cannot come..."[69] After this revelation, he commanded they love one another as a sign that they were his disciples.

At the news that Jesus was leaving, Simon Peter immediately felt a surge of distress, as if struck by a bolt of lightening in his spirit. For nearly three years, he and the others had followed the Lord believing him to be the Messiah foretold in the scriptures. They had been by his side, seen his miracles, heard his astounding words, and rejoiced in the delights of his divine fellowship. Because of him, their lives had been changed. And without him they would be helpless, like children lost in their way. Peter aroused, spoke up, "Lord, where are you going?"[70]

"Where I am going," replied Jesus, "you cannot follow me now; but you shall follow me afterwards."[71]

Shocked into persistence Peter wanted to know, "Why can't I follow you now? I'd lay down my life for you." Peter didn't understand the cross; neither did the other disciples. Perhaps there was even a sense of mild anger, that after so long a time following Jesus, he would leave Peter behind. "The others, yes, but not me; I'm Simon Peter, the Rock. I'm ready to die for you." Peter always had a problem with pride, and Jesus pointed this out when he challenged his faithfulness unto death: "Will you lay down your life for my sake? Verily, verily, I say into you, the cock shall not crow, till you have denied me three times."

To calm their distress, Jesus left them this beautiful promise of assurance:

> *"Let not your heart be troubled: Ye believe in God, believe also in me. In My Father's house are many mansions: If it were not so, I would have told you. I go to prepare a place for you. And if I go and prepare a place for you, I will come again, and receive you unto myself; that where I am, there ye may be also."*[72]

It was time for the Lord Jesus to exit this realm of existence. The work of the cross lay ahead. His redemptive work on behalf of mankind would soon be finished. He was going home, going home as a human being, the first of our kind to venture into the forbidden, eternal land of Almighty God. Once there, the rest of our kind, ransomed from sin by the atoning merits of Jesus Christ, could claim the assurances of being bound for the Promised Land.

Hope for Troubled Hearts

First, you will need the comfort, peace, and assurance that after death, *a place* has been prepared for your eternal habitation. Jesus said, "Let not your heart be troubled..."

Again, the shadow of the cross was falling upon the Lord Jesus. And it was in the awareness, that his death was eminent, when Jesus gave to his disciples the comfort of a better day coming. He knew they would be troubled in their hearts without his earthly Presence. He wanted them to be comforted. His death would not be the end of Him. In fact, his death was a new beginning, not only for the disciples but for all who believe.

What you believe about Christ, to say the least, is important. Maybe you haven't thought about it, but Jesus Christ is the first of our kind to rise from the dead. If that is not so, you and I have no rhyme or reason why we were even born. No significance. No ultimate meaning in our life-cycle. One generation will pass and another rises. But why this hopeless Bataan death marches to nowhere?

Someone has rightly observed that the sum total of human life is in three momentous occasions: We are hatched, matched, and dispatched. That is, we are born, we marry, we work, have children, and then we die. And so the question is, "Is this all there is to life?" Not if you believe that Jesus Christ rose from the dead. The Christ, though garbed in flesh and blood, is still God who came to give us the hope of a new beginning.

Think about a new beginning. Since there is a human being who has overcome death, the implication for the rest of humanity is that there is hope after death. A new beginning is eminent. Our bodies though they are sown in corruption, will be raised in incorruption. For the people of faith though our bodies are dishonored, they will be raised in glory. Sown in weakness, they will be raised in power. Sown a natural body, they will be raised a spiritual body.[73] Cessation of our earthly existence is the beginning of a new and heavenly life realized only in Jesus Christ.[74]

Let's all agree, if there is one thing that troubles us most of all, it is the subject of death. No one wants to die. No one really looks forward to the end of this earthly journey. After all, this is the only life we've ever known. And yet, death is eminent and undeniable. We know this experientially. People die. They die all the time. Everyday thousands of our kinds exit this world to meet their Maker.

The Bible addresses issues of and life and death. The scriptures alert us that, "It is appointed unto men once to die, but after this the judgement."[75] But the Bible also reminds us that Jesus came that we might have life and have it more abundantly.[76] This is tremendous news. And yet, in this life, you cannot have one without the other, life without death. It is the way of all flesh. And we can't say that we were not warned. God alerted Adam:

> *"...of every tree of the garden thou may freely eat: But of the tree of the knowledge of good and evil, thou shalt not eat: for in the day that thou eatest thereof, thou shalt surely die."*[77]

But right here, is why we need the comfort of an untroubled heart. Why we need a new beginning. The Bible lets us know that the last enemy of humanity is death.[78] In The Book of The Revelation, we are informed that in the New Heaven and New Earth there shall be no more death.[79] Paul, the great Apostle of Christ, rejoiced to say, "O wretched man that I am! Who shall deliver me from this body of death? I thank God through Jesus Christ our Lord."[80] Paul recognized and understood Christ to be the great liberator of death, hell, and the grave. Throughout the Bible there is this tremendous assurance of comfort that once we depart these earthly bodies we are free to journey into the presence of our Maker.[81] To enter this spiritual realm we will need spiritual bodies. "Flesh and blood cannot enter the Kingdom of God," Paul said, "Neither doth corruption inherit incorruption."[82] And so, when Jesus said, "Let not your hearts be troubled," he was offering you and me the assurance and comfort of the Father's House. He wanted us to know that death is only the beginning of life, not the end.

Have you made your reservation? Is your soul at peace with your Maker? I mean, if you died right now, do you have the assurance of your soul's eternal estate? It's really not that difficult to claim the comfort of Christ. It is simply a matter of *soul preparation*. The Bible makes it clear that one's salvation is initiated in a step of faith:

> *"For by grace are ye saved through faith; and that not of yourselves: it is the gift of God: Not of works, lest any man should boast."*[83]

It is a matter of calling upon Christ for the forgiveness of your sins.[84] You can see from the above passage that the method of salvation is clear: Faith in Jesus Christ for the forgiveness of sin. We cannot have eternal life and heaven without God's prescribed means of securing it.

What does it take to get to heaven and secure your eternal estate? Let us use Faith (**F**orsaking **A**ll **I** **T**ake **H**im) as an acrostic to make clear God's plan of salvation:

> *#1: F is for forgiveness. We cannot have eternal life and heaven without God's forgiveness. In him (meaning Jesus) we have redemption through his blood, the forgiveness of our sins"* (Ephesians 1:7).
>
> *#2: A is for available. Forgiveness is available for all. "For God so loved the world that he gave his only begotten Son that whosoever believeth in him should not perish, but have everlasting life" (John 3:16).*
>
> *#3: I is for impossible. It is impossible for God to allow sin into Heaven. "For all have sinned And come short of the glory of God" (Romans 3:23).*
>
> *#4: T is for Turn. Turn means repent. We must turn from sin and self. "But unless you repent, you will all perish" (Luke 13:3).*
>
> *#5: H is for heaven. Heaven is eternal life. "If I go away and prepare a place for you, I will come again and receive you unto Myself"(John 14:3).*

One of the dear ladies in our church asked me, "Do you know what Bible means?"

"I do," I remarked. "It means Book."

"No, no, no," she replied. "Do you really know what it means?"

"Please. You tell me what the word Bible means."

With a Cheshire cat's grin, she said, "it means, 'Basic Instructions before Leaving Earth.'"

I thought, "I couldn't have said it any better myself." It's so true. The Bible is indeed God's instruction manual on how to get saved and get to heaven.

Do not believe the devil's lie that death is painless extinction. Life has been lent to you and has a divine purpose. You need to cherish life and use it wisely to the glory of God. And because life is a gift from God you can be assured there is a "payday, someday." Everyone ends up somewhere after the event of death. When your life is coming to physical closure, you do not have to be troubled and comfortless. The Presence of God is all you need. Always remember, God does love you and desires that you love him. And he wants you to know it is okay. When death comes, you will not be alone.[85] Be comforted. In Christ, it is safe to give up this body of death and move to higher ground.[86]

But there are the "soul gamblers" who willingly wage that there is no God and death is the end of existence. In Dr. Maurice Rawlings's book, "Beyond Death's Door," he tells the story of a 48-year-old, white male who had cardiac arrest while doing an EKG. His heart completely stopped functioning as he collapsed to the floor in a lifeless heap. Immediately Dr. Maurice started CPR:

> *"The patient began 'coming to.' But whenever I would reach for instruments or otherwise interrupt my compression of his chest, the patient would again lose consciousness,*

> *roll his eyes upward, arch his back in mild convulsions, stop breathing, and die once more. Each time he regained heartbeat and respiration, the patient screamed,'I am in hell!' He was terrified and pleaded with me to help him. I was scared to death. In fact, this episode literally scared the hell out of me. He then issued a very strange plea: 'Don't stop!... Don't you understand? I am in hell. Each time you quit I go back to hell. Don't let me go back to hell.'...After several death episodes he finally asked me, 'How do I stay out of hell?' I told him I guessed it was the same principle learned in Sunday School——that I guessed Jesus Christ would be the one whom you would ask to save you. Then he said, 'I don't know how to pray. Pray for me.' I told him that I was a doctor, not a preacher. 'Pray for me,' he repeated."*[87]

It was a dying man's request. Although Dr. Maurice was not a Christian at the time, he asked the man to repeat a prayer that went something like this:

> "Lord Jesus, I ask you to keep me out of hell. Forgive me of my sins. I turn my life over to you. If I die, I want to go to heaven. If I live, I'll be 'on the hook' forever."[88]

The man lived and became a compelling witness for Jesus Christ. As for Dr. Maurice, he was discovering that the Bible was not merely a history book. Every word was turning out to be true. He decided he had better start reading it very closely.[89]

The man who clinically died and found himself in hell was anything, but comforted. His heart was troubled, fearfully so.

You say, "Well, he was simply beside himself; or probably having hallucinations. I'll wager this man was not in his right mind."

Fine, be a "soul-gambler." Go ahead and wager there is no heaven or hell. Believe that the Bible is just a book of ancient fiction, full of myths. Go right ahead. Believe when this life is over you simply cease to exist. But what if you are wrong? What if Jesus Christ is "Emmanuel," God with us? What then?

Last night I was called to a home. The daughter requested I come. Her father was dying and she was unsure of his salvation. I sat by the bed of an 84-year-old man who had recently been told he only had a couple of weeks. We spoke for a while. I took his hand and asked, "Tom, are you prepared to meet God?"

In a raspy voice, he replied, "Best I can be, I guess."

"Let's talk to the Lord," I said, "and make sure."

He agreed and we prayed. Afterwards, there was a comfort for both he and family that his departure from this life was secure in the promises of God.

There is comfort for troubled hearts. Jesus said, "Let not your hearts be troubled…"

Reserved For God's People

Heaven is reserved for those who have believing faith in Jesus Christ. Jesus said, "…ye believe in God, believe also in me." Faith is a powerful tool in the spiritual realm. Faith gives you an answer when you wonder, "where is God when it hurts," or "where is God when I walk through the fire." Faith is a clarion call that invites the great God of heaven and earth to give you courage in the calamities of life.[90] Faith will let you know that you are not alone.[91] But the most necessary faith is "believing faith," a faith that believes that Jesus Christ is very God and that His promises are true.[92] Sinners can be assured that heaven is real by taking Jesus Christ at His Word.[93]

Jesus said, "If you believe in God, believe also in me." This is a powerful claim. Some would even say an outlandish claim. And yet we would recognize in this phrase an avowed equality by Jesus Christ as one with God the Creator.[94] This is astounding. Here is a human being, a flesh and blood creature, attributing to himself a special relationship with the transcendent and eternal God of the ages. Which by implication suggest, here is more than a mere man. Indeed, Jesus Christ is more than a man.[95] He is the Son of God and Savior of mankind.[96] He is the Resurrection and the Life.[97] But without "faith" these provocative truths cannot be personalized. And if they are not personalized, neither can they be utilized.

Faith is the key that appropriates the awareness of God's presence in our rogue events.[98] We must not be blinded to the importance of Faith: Faith literally defines what we are in the sight of a holy God (Christ-righteous, or self-righteousness), and what destiny awaits each after death (Heaven, or hell).[99]

In this present life, we operate by physical sight. We would all agree that to be physically blind would indeed be a serious handicap. And so in this physical world, we need physical sight. Likewise, in the spiritual realm, we need spiritual sight. The Bible calls this spiritual sight, "...the eyes of your understanding..."[100] When the light of God's Truth is received by faith, like candlelight in the corner of a dark room, the darkness of ignorance recedes. Fear flees. And even in a "sky falling" we can find comfort by trusting the Lord. Even in a rogue event there is faith for a heart that believes.

William Barclay commented on John 14:1-3:

> *"There comes a time when we have to believe where we cannot prove and to accept where we cannot understand. If, in the darkest hour, we believe that somehow there is a purpose in life and that that purpose is love, even the unbearable becomes bearable and even in the darkness there is a glimmer of life."*[101]

The disciples were about to experience their darkest hour. For nearly three years they had committed their lives to the one whom they believed to be the Son of God. Never had they felt as alive as in the presence of Jesus. But now they hear the unthinkable announcement that He would soon be leaving.

Earlier Jesus had informed the disciples that his time upon the earth was nearing its conclusion. The cross was looming like a long, dark, shadow. It was time for him to fulfill the purpose for which he had been born: To give his life a ransom for many.[102] It was now, in their darkest hour, that he would leave them a glimmer of light saying, "Let not your hearts be troubled: Ye believe in God, believe also in Me."

It's not easy to accept what we cannot comprehend; to hold fast to faith in a rogue storm, a sky falling. And yet without lashing ourselves to this tried and true mast we call faith, trusting in the Christ who is able to calm the storms with a gentle whisper, how shall we prevail? "For if you believe not that I am he," Jesus said, "you shall die in your sins."[103]

Faith for a believing heart is to be had only in Jesus Christ. He said: "Ye believe in God, believe also in me." Have you received your place in heaven? Heaven is a place reserved for those who trust Christ for the forgiveness of their sins.

This Promise Kept

Once this life is over, is there really something else, another habitat that awaits those who believe God? Jesus said:

> "In My Father's House are many mansions:
> If it were not so, I would have told you. I go
> to prepare a place for you."[104]

He told his disciples that in his Father's House there are many mansions (literally: Abiding places), places to take up one's heavenly residence. Hear the honesty of our Lord's words, "If it were not so, I would have told you." So, we are to be patient as he has gone to prepare this special place. His is a promise to be kept.

This promise kept is a promise of comfort for troubled hearts: "Let not your heart be troubled..."

This promise kept is a promise of faith for believing hearts: "...ye believe in God, believe also in me. In My Father's House are many mansions: If it were not so, I would have told you..."

This promise kept is a promise of hope for patient hearts: "I go to prepare a place for you." Some have said there is nothing sure, but death and taxes. Yet, The Bible tells us that God cannot lie. Since Jesus Christ is God, it is not possible for him to tell a falsehood. Let us be mindful that Jesus said himself, "I am the way, the truth, and the life..."[105] He is the truth of God. In John's Gospel we are told, "For the law was given by Moses, but grace and truth came by Jesus Christ."[106] If Jesus said that he has gone ahead to prepare a place for you, then believe what he has promised. Settle the matter right now! His is a promise to be kept because his is a sure promise.

This promise kept is a promise of joy for watching hearts: "And if I go and prepare a place for you, I will come again, and receive you unto myself; that where I am, there you may be also."

Some people could care less about heaven. Or, hell for that matter! Such places, they reason, have been conjured only in the minds of superstitious men. Yet, when you consider what the Lord Jesus said about heaven, you are led to believe that he had a constant sense of life beyond earth. When Pilate confronted Jesus, if he were a king, our Lord responded: "My kingdom is not of this world..."[107] In one of our Lord's prayers, he said, "...I am not of this world."[108] And as we have already mentioned Jesus on the eve of his crucifixion told his disciples, "...I go to prepare a place fore you."[109] Jesus knew from whence he had come: He is as the scriptures identify, "...the Lord from heaven."[110]

Perhaps, we should not be so quick to dismiss what we cannot see, or choose not to believe. Simple logic lets us know there is a heaven and a hell. Logic dictates that there are diametrically opposing extremes in life. So, why should it be any different in the spiritual realm? If there is a heaven, there must be a hell. Remember, just because we couldn't see atoms, didn't mean they were nonexistent. But it is not logic that convinces us of the reality of heaven. It is a matter of faith, of trusting Jesus Christ at His word. After all, he told us with such refreshing honesty, "...if it were not so, I would have told you. I go to prepare a place for you."[111]

Heaven is a "faith-choice." Once you accept Jesus Christ, "By grace...through faith," as a gift from God, heaven becomes a real future destiny.[112] The necessity of this *faith-choice* cannot be overemphasized. When one chooses to discover who Jesus Christ is, then he/she is enabled by the Spirit of God to discover and know God.[113] God became one of us, a human being, so we could discover him in human flesh. And when you discover God in Christ, then something wonderful occurs inside our darkened souls: The eyes of our understanding are enlightened.[114] At this point it is possible to discern spiritual things; hence, heaven makes sense and becomes a thrilling hope in the life of the believer.

The Coke Company used to have a clever jingle some years back. When they advertised their product, someone would sing, "It's the real thing." The Coca-Cola people wanted the whole world to know that their soda was different from all the rest; that it was the real thing!

The ultimate authority on heaven is the Bible. And the Bible tells us that heaven is a real place; that is, it is a real and tangible piece of property. The Lord Jesus called heaven "a place." He said: "In My Father's House are many mansions...I go to prepare a place for you."[115]

Is heaven a myth, a fantasy, or wishful thinking? According to Jesus heaven is a real place. He told his disciples not to worry about death[116] and gave them a reason why: "In my Father's House are many mansions; if it were not so, I would have told you. I go to prepare a place for you."[117]

Just because you can't see heaven doesn't mean it's not a real place. The Manhattan Project where the atomic bomb was developed was an act of believing what one could not see. No one had ever seen an atom. President Roosevelt reportedly asked Albert Einstein if he's ever seen an atom to which he responded; "No we have not." Einstein's placed faith in his theories and the moment arrived when that which was not seen became a reality.

Heaven is a real place and in Revelation 21, we are told a number of things about heaven:

> *In heaven there is no more sea: "...and there was no more sea."[118] This means that in heaven there is nothing that separates.*
>
> *In heaven there is no more tears: "And God shall wipe away all tears from their eyes..."[119] In heaven there is nothing that will sadden or bring sorrow.*

> *In heaven there is no more death: "...and there shall be no more death..."*[120] *There will be no grief in heaven.*
>
> *In heaven there will be no more pain: "...neither shall there be any more pain..."*[121] *No one hurts in heaven.*
>
> *In heaven there is no more sin: "And there shall in no wise enter into it any thing that defiles..."*[122] *No one is unholy in heaven.*
>
> *In heaven there is no more night: "...for there shall be no night there." Nothing to fear.*[123]

In heaven there will be no ambulances, police stations, standing military, funerals, obituaries, cemeteries, hospitals, broken marriages, bruised hearts, divided homes, or abused children. Life as we know it will be a thing of the past. And he that sits upon the throne of heaven will say: "Behold, I make all things new."

Conclusion

We live in an insecure world. The road of life is littered with the pot-holes of crippling trials and tribulations. At any moment, like an explosive device, these trials may explode and wreak havoc. Like a sky falling, our lives are threatened to shatter in a million pieces. No hope. No refuge. Such is the aftermath of a "rogue day." It is never "if" but only "when." And preparation is paramount.

Preparation means submitting your life and your plight to the Lordship of Jesus Christ. Only he can be your sin-bearer, there are no others. Submission is the key to overcoming a rogue day. When your sky is falling, pray and call upon God to give you the joy of His presence, an understanding mind, a surrendered will, and a heart that wants to believe. In him you are no longer a victim, but as Paul said: "...we are more than conquerors through him who first loved us."[124]

Go out and conquer your rogue day. And remember, you are not alone in the battles of life. The Christ of Calvary's Hill is you Conquering Captain. The banner of his cross is the guarantee of your triumph. You don't run to victory, you run from victory. At Calvary's crimson cross the triumphant cry of our Mighty Deliverer, "It is finished" shook the dark pits of hell's domain and blasted down the prison gates. The power of sin has been broken once and far all.

Submit to His Lordship.
Be a conqueror.
Be victorious.
In him you need never fear a sky falling.

The end

End Notes

Introduction: Sky Falling: How to Overcome A Rogue Day

[1] Ephesians 6:12
[2] Isaiah 53:5
[3] Genesis 3:15
[4] Job 16:33
[5] John 14:18
[6] Sebastain Junger, <u>The Perfect Storm</u> (New York: Harper Perennial, 1999), p.122.
[7] Ibid., p.122.
[8] Ibid., p.122.
[9] Ibid., p.123.
[10] Ibid., p.123.
[11] 1Thessalonians 5:23
[12] Luke 22:44
[13] Nehemiah 8:10
[14] Psalms 139:14
[15] 2Kings 20:7

[16] Mark 4:39
[17] Acts 10:40
[18] Amos 4:12
[19] Luke 13:5
[20] Colossians 1:14
[21] Mark 1:15
[22] Job 1:12
[23] Genesis 2:16-17
[24] 1Corinthians 15:21-22
[25] Genesis 3:24
[26] Luke 23:43
[27] Luke 13:5
[28] Bill Hancock, <u>Riding With The Blue Moth</u> (Champion, Il.: Sports Publishing L.L.C., 2005), p.13.
[29] Ibid., p.13.
[30] Ibid., p.13.
[31] Ibid., p.245.
[32] Psalms 27:9
[33] 2Timothy 4:10-11,14,16
[34] 2Timothy 4:17
[35] John MacAuthor, Jr., <u>The Power Of Suffering</u> (Wheaton, Il.: Victor Books, 1995), p.148
[36] James 4:7

Chapter 1
[1] Nehemiah 8:10
[2] James 1:2
[3] John 16:33
[4] Acts 14:22
[5] Acts 9:6

[6] Acts 9:16
[7] 2Corinthians 11:23-27
[8] 2Timothy 2:9
[9] Acts 16:25
[10] Matthew 16:29
[11] Hebrews 12:2
[12] Matthew 26:41
[14] Matthew 26:38
[15] Luke 22:44
[16] Pierre Barbet, M.D., <u>A Doctor At Calvary</u> (Garden City, New York: Image Books Edition, 1963), p.48.
[17] Matthew 27:32
[18] Matthew 26:39
[19] Isaiah 53:5
[20] Hebrews 12:2
[21] Philippians 1:29
[22] 1Peter 5:8
[23] James 1:1
[24] Romans 9:4
[25] Romans 9:6
[26] Romans 9:7-8
[27] John 3:7
[28] Acts 1:8
[29] Matthew 13:19
[30] 1Peter 5:8
[31] 1John 2:16
[32] Genesis 3:5-6
[33] Job 2:1-6
[34] Job 2:1
[35] Job 2:3
[36] Job 2:6

[37] 2Corinthians 12:9;Hebrews 13:5
[38] James 4:14
[39] 1Peter 4:12
[40] Luke 10:30
[41] James 4:14
[42] Job 8:9
[43] Job 9:22
[44] Job 14:1-22
[45] Psalms 39:5
[46] 1Peter 1:24
[47] Stephen Cherniske,M.S.,The Metabolic Plan (New York, N.Y.: Ballentine Books, 2004), p.1
[48] Jo 16:33
[49] James 1:2
[50] Matthew 1:23
[51] Hebrews 13:5
[52] Genesis 28:1
[53] Exodus 33:14
[54] Philippians 3:8
[55] John 15:11

Chapter 2
[1] Ephesians 2:12
[2] Hebrews 12:5
[3] 1Corinthians 10:10
[4] Jonah 4:3
[5] John 16:33
[6] Genesis 2:17
[7] Steven Cherniske, The Metabolic Plan (New York: Ballentine Books, 2004), p.21.
[8] Hebrews 12:11

[9] James 1:3
[10] James 1:3
[11] Genesis 22:1-2
[12] Deuteronomy 8:2
[13] 1Kings 3:5
[14] Psalms 7:9
[15] John 6:5-6
[16] John 11:6
[17] Franklin Graham, <u>Rebel With A Cause</u> (Nashville, Tenn.: Thomas Nelson Publishers,1995),p.139.
[18] Ibid., 141.
[19] Luke 22:31-32
[20] Exodus 14:13
[21] Philippians 1:29
[22] Acts 16:23-24
[23] James 1:2-3
[24] Matthew 4
[25] Hebrews 5:8-9
[26] 1Peter 1:7
[27] 2Corinthians 4:17
[28] James 1:3
[29] Romans 5:3-4
[30] 2Timothy 2:15
[31] 2Timothy 2:16
[32] 1Corinthians 11:28
[33] Genesis 3:5
[34] Judges 21:25
[35] 2Samuel 12:10-12
[36] 2Samuel 12:13

Chapter 3

[1] Hebrews 12:2
[2] John 13:36
[3] Matthew 26:42
[4] John 4:34
[5] John 6:38-40
[6] John 19:30
[7] Psalms 121:1-8
[8] Acts 14:22
[9] James 1:4
[10] Jonah 1:17
[11] Romans 8:29
[12] Colossians 1:27
[13] James 1:4
[14] Hebrews 11:6
[15] Ephesians 2:8-9
[16] Ephesians 2:10a/Romans 8:29
[17] Ephesians 2:10b

Chapter 4

[1] James 4:3/5:13-16
[2] Proverbs 15:14
[3] Philippians 4:7
[4] James 1:5
[5] 1Chronicles 16:11
[6] Luke 18:1
[7] Luke 22:44
[8] Ephesians 6:18
[9] Psalms 46:19

[10] James 1:5
[11] James 1:6-8
[12] Luke 1:37
[13] Hebrews 11:6
[14] 1John 5:14
[15] James 1:6b
[16] James 1:7
[17] James 1:8
[18] James 1:12

Chapter 5

[1] 1Peter 1:3
[2] Revelation 20:6/John 3:7
[3] Hebrews 9:27-28
[4] Genesis 2:17
[5] Stephen Cherniske, <u>The Metabolic Plan</u> (New York: Ballentine Books, 2004), p.1.
[6] Romans 7:24-25
[7] James 4:14
[8] 2Corinthians 5:8
[9] 2Timothy 3:16
[10] 1Thessalonians 5:23
[11] Ezekiel 18:4/Romans 6:23
[12] Genesis 2:7
[13] John 4:24
[14] 2 Corinthians 5:10
[15] Luke 16:26
[16] 2Corinthians 5:10
[17] 2Corinthians 5:10/Romans 14:10
[18] Romans 8:1

[19] 1Corinthians 3:8/Matthew 16:27
[20] John 3:16
[21] 2Corinthians 5:21
[22] Hebrews 9:26
[23] Matthew 25:23
[24] Revelation 20:11-15
[25] John 14:3
[26] Mark 9:46
[27] Hebrews 7:25-26
[28] 1John 2:1-2
[29] 1Peter 3:18
[30] John 6:68
[31] Ezekiel 18:4,20
[32] John 8:21,24
[33] Hebrews 9:22
[34] Romans 5:6-11/1John 2:2
[35] Titus 2:13-14
[36] 1John 3:3
[37] 2Peter 3:11
[38] Job 19:25
[39] Zechariah 14:3-4,9
[40] Psalms 102:16
[41] Daniel 2:34-39
[42] Isaiah 9:6-7
[43] Luke 21:26-27
[44] John 14:3
[45] Revelation 22:20
[46] Matthew 7:15-20
[47] Revelation 19:16
[48] Matthew 24:37-41
[49] 1Thessalonians 4:16-17
[50] Revelation 14:19

[51] Revelation 19:15-16

Chapter 6

[1] John 16:21
[2] John 16:22
[3] Philip Yancy, <u>Where Is God When It Hurts?</u> (Grand Rapids, Michigan: Zondervon Publishers, 1977),p.179.
[4] Ibid.,p.179.
[5] Ibid.,p.180.
[6] Ibid.,p.180.
[7] Matthew 25:21/Revelation 21:5
[8] Romans 8:37

Chapter 7

[1] John 14:1-3
[2] Genesis 3:5
[3] 1Corinthian 2:9
[4] Titus 1:1-2
[5] William J. Federer, <u>America's God and Country</u> (Coppell, Texas, Fame Publishing, Inc.,1994) p.113
[6] Ibid., p.
[7] John 13:33, 36;14:3
[8] Hebrews 7:25-28; 1Timothy 2:5
[9] Hebrews 11:10
[10] Psalms 139:14
[11] Genesis 2:7
[12] Genesis 1:27

[13] Genesis 13:1
[14] Genesis 12:2
[15] Genesis 11:8
[16] Genesis 11:10
[17] Genesis 15:18
[18] John 3:3
[19] John 4:16
[20] John 8:24
[21] John 11:25
[22] Hebrews 9:27-28
[23] Matthew 7:13-14
[24] Matthew 7:13
[26] Proverbs 12:12
[27] Hebrews 11:8
[28] Hebrews 11:8
[29] Genesis 12:2
[30] John 14:1-3
[31] 1Corinthians 2:9
[32] Ephesians 2:8
[33] Hebrews 11:11-12
[34] Genesis 12:2
[35] Jeremiah 29:11
[36] Romans 10:9
[37] John 14:3
[38] Galatians 5:22-23
[39] Psalms 27:14
[40] Genesis 16:2
[41] Genesis 16:12
[42] Hebrews 11:13-16
[43] Genesis 12:3
[44] Hebrews 11:13
[45] Hebrews 6:19

[46] Don Piper, <u>90 Minutes In Heaven</u> (Grand Rapids, Michigan, Revell Publishers, 2004), p.21.
[47] Genesis 50:24:26
[48] Hebrews 11:17-19
[49] John 3:16
[50] Hebrews 5:8
[51] Hebrews 11:6
[52] Matthew 16:16
[53] Hebrews 12:14
[54] John 14:3
[55] John 12:26
[56] John 17:24
[57] Ron Chernow, <u>Alexander Hamilton</u>(New York: N.Y., Penguin Press, 2004), p.707.
[58] 1John 2:2
[59] John 18:37
[60] Hebrews 5:8
[61] John 17:4-5
[62] Matthew 1:21
[63] John 8:23
[64] John 18:36
[65] Psalms 24
[66] Zechariah 13:6
[67] John 17:22
[68] Tom Fettke, Editor, <u>The Hymnal For Worship And Celebration</u> (Waco, Texas: Word Music, 1986), p. 552.
[69] John 13:33
[70] John 13:36
[71] John 13:16
[72] John 14:1-3
[73] 1Corinthians 15:44

[74] 2Corinthians 5:8
[75] Hebrews 9:27
[76] John 10:10
[77] Genesis 2:16-17
[78] 1Corinthians 15:26
[79] Revelation 21:4
[80] Romans 7:24
[81] 2Corinthians 5:8
[82] 1Corthinians 15:20
[83] Ephesians 2:8
[84] Romans 10:13
[85] Matthew 28:20
[86] Romans 7:24-25
[87] Maurice Rawlings, M.D., Beyond Death's Door (Nashville, Tenn., Thomas Nelson Inc., 1978), pp.17-18.
[88] Ibid., p.19.
[89] Ibid., p. 20.
[90] Isaiah 65:24
[91] Hebrews 13:5
[92] Ephesians 2:8
[93] Acts 4:12
[94] John 5:18; Philippians 2:6
[95] Philippians 2:9-11
[96] Luke 1:32
[97] John 11:25
[98] 1John 5:4
[99] Luke 16:19-20
[100] Ephesians 1:18
[101] William Barclay, The Gospel of John, Vol.2, (Philadelphia, Penn., The Westminister Press, 1976), pp. 152-153.

[102] Mark 10:45
[103] John 8:24
[104] John 14:2
[105] John 14:6
[106] John 1:17
[107] John 18:36
[108] John 17:14, 16
[109] John 14:3
[110] 1Corinthians 15:47
[111] John 14:2
[112] Ephesians 2:8-9
[113] John 16:13-1

About The Author

Paul Roland lives in Mobile, Alabama, with his beautiful wife of 37-years, Cynthia. They have four grown children, John, James, Michael, and Leah of whom they are very proud. Presently, Dr. Paul pastors The Snow Road First Baptist Church in Semmes, Alabama.

Printed in the United States
130872LV00001B/207/P